Susan Feniger's

STREET
FOOD

Susan Feniger's STREET FOOD

Irresistibly Crispy, Creamy, Crunchy, Spicy, Sticky, Sweet Recipes

SUSAN FENIGER WITH **KAJSA ALGER** AND **LIZ LACHMAN**
PHOTOGRAPHS BY **JENNIFER MAY**

CLARKSON POTTER/PUBLISHERS
New York

Copyright © 2012 by Susan Feniger
Photographs copyright © 2012 by Jennifer May

All rights reserved.
Published in the United States by Clarkson Potter/Publishers,
an imprint of the Crown Publishing Group, a division of
Random House, Inc., New York.
www.crownpublishing.com
www.clarksonpotter.com

CLARKSON POTTER is a trademark and POTTER with colophon
is a registered trademark of Random House, Inc.

Library of Congress Cataloging-in-Publication Data
is available upon request.

ISBN 978-0-307-95258-5

Printed in China

Design by Stephanie Huntwork

10 9 8 7 6 5 4 3 2 1

First Edition

This book is dedicated to the memory of my
mother and father. They not only gave me
life but also taught me how to love it.

CONTENTS

INTRODUCTION

MY FIRST LOVE has always been food. But in the search for ever more interesting and challenging cuisines, I discovered my second love: learning about people and their cultures. Nothing pleases me more than to travel in some foreign place, stop at a little stand on the street for some amazing dish I've never heard of, and suddenly find myself engaged in a conversation with a complete stranger. I believe that in any country, what you see and taste on the street is the best food you'll find, because it's usually one family's recipe handed down and perfected over generations. There aren't any frills; there's no service; all the focus is on the food.

Only at a street stand, barely speaking the same language, can you start out as a customer and end up invited home to cook with the chef's mother or grandmother. I have been taught so many recipes and learned so many styles of cooking, and often my only form of communication has been our common language of food. As we cook, I learn. All over the world, I've seen the same beauty of culture and people, of simplicity blended with spirituality, warmth, and artistry. And it always comes together around food on the street or in someone's home kitchen.

Opening Susan Feniger's STREET in Los Angeles was like trying to capture lightning in a bottle. That indefinable "magical" street experience is what I wanted to re-create. It meant that, in doing something unique and delicious in the spirit of street food, I also had to create the warmth and friendliness that marked part of that mystical experience of a street stand in a foreign country. So I set to work with Kajsa Alger—partner in and executive chef at STREET—to try to accomplish the task. And I think we did! Now our best nights at STREET are when strangers from neighboring tables strike up conversations about the food and sometimes even pull up chairs and share dishes.

I want to give you, the home cook, the chance to get your God-given tools for mixing—called "hands"—dirty. There's no daintiness in street cooking; there's rolling up your sleeves and getting involved in a new culture with brand-new flavors and lots of joy. "World cuisine" sounds exotic and difficult, but once you learn the basics, it's fairly simple.

Yes, you will be pushed to expand. No question. But honestly, aren't we all sick of making the same dishes over and over, mac 'n' cheese and blueberry muffins aside? This is my chance to share the burning curiosity that has been my driving force. And it's my invitation for you to step onto the wild side, learning totally new recipes and styles from the streets of Ho Chi Minh

City to the streets of Kochi, India. Everything from all countries is on the table. (Sorry for the pun.)

I'll share kitchen tips and techniques I've picked up along the way in my thirty years of cooking and traveling, and I'll tell stories about some of my most favorite travel moments, and my hope is that by the end of our time together you will know me better and will have a brand-new bag of tricks for kitchen techniques. Maybe you'll even be inspired to take your own street food tour to some exotic place!

One thing you should know: I love to play with my food, so everything in this book is geared toward supporting you to do the same. Have a blast and enjoy!

ORGANIZING
THE WORLD'S KITCHEN

COOKING WITH new spices and unfamiliar ingredients from different cultures can sometimes feel like wandering in the wilderness. The thing to remember is this: Taste is universal. It doesn't matter what country or culture you are exploring, salt is still salty, sugar is still sweet. Different cultures use different ingredients to accomplish the very same tasks. Once you understand that and get to know those ingredients, finding your way around international cuisines becomes much less mysterious.

In looking at how the kitchens of the world are organized, you can see that there are more similarities than differences. The goal is to feel less lost and more in command when you're cooking with the myriad ingredients that global cuisine has to offer. You will gradually learn how to taste for balance and create it as you broaden your knowledge of this "language" of ingredients. When you become fluent is when the real mystery deepens—and the adventure begins.

Most of the flavors in the lists below need one or more flavors from the other lists to balance them. The key is to know that each flavor does something different on your tongue and to learn how to combine the ingredients. The blend is what counts. That's why I stress balance so much. It's my way of cooking well.

THE SALTS

Soy sauce. Tamari. Fish sauce. Brines. Achiote. Miso. Dried shrimp. Anchovies. Capers.

Salt is a flavor that people are hesitant to use because it can seem overpowering. But without salt, dishes taste flat and the other flavors don't reach their full potential. Salt makes every other flavor sing. It can be such a beautiful complement when it comes in the form of something like a dark Malaysian soy sauce in a seafood dish, or ground dried shrimp in a Nigerian sauce or Brazilian fritter. Fish sauce makes a crisp, clean Vietnamese spring roll pop with brightness. For example, in the United States we're just beginning to become familiar with the many different types, textures, colors, and flavors of all the varieties of sea salt, and that's still just in the form of rock salts! Remember, the depth of flavor in a dish doesn't come from the laundry list of ingredients, but from the balance that is created by the combination of those ingredients.

THE SOURS
Pickles. Vinegars. Umeboshi plums. Citrus. Rose hips. Tamarind. Hibiscus. Yuzu. Fermented grains. Wines.

All over the world, sour is the flavor that brings brightness to something that's too rich. It's why pickles and hamburgers, salsa and guacamole, chutney and yogurt, lime and coconut all go so well together. Interestingly, the intensity of the sour flavor can be changed. When you slowly cook and reduce a sour ingredient, something like balsamic vinegar or citrus juice can actually turn sweet. The world's "sours" will lead you to discover startling new characteristics of flowers, pods, fruits, fermented legumes, and grains, and will bring you into a deeper understanding of how to combine flavors and bring depth and complexity to a dish.

THE SWEETS
Palm sugars. Onion. Maple. Sorghum. Molasses. Dates. Syrups. Blossom waters. Honey. Dried fruits.

Different parts of the world and various cultures have been coming up with ingenious ways to sweeten their food for centuries. In the United States, we've grown used to the sweetness of refined sugar and corn syrup, which definitely has its limitations. The truth is there is a rainbow of "sweet" out there in the world. When a puree of plumped raisins or dates is added to a tamarind chutney from India, that great natural fruity sweetness you taste is fresh and clean; when a Turkish cake is dipped in a warm syrup of blossom water and honey, you are transported to an exotic place by the delicate floral aromas that are so much more subtle than what you experience in processed candy. The richness of molasses, the grassiness of sorghum and caramelized onion, the toasted nuttiness of carob syrup, and the lightness of dried apricot: these are the earthy, natural, global "sweets" I am excited for you to discover.

THE HOT AND SPICY
Chiles. Ginger. Mustards. Cinnamon. Peppercorns. Garlic. Black cardamom.

Without heat and spice, three-quarters of the world would be lost. It's what gives so many dishes their character. At the same time, although I love a "kick," I never want my food to be all about the heat or how much spiciness one can tolerate, because I'm more interested in how the flavors blend and finish on the palate. The spices on this list are incredibly diverse in heat, color, flavor, and earthiness. Chiles alone have so many wonderful varieties and sub-varieties; it's an exciting adventure just to discover them all. That's what's so exhilarating about the "hot and spicy" in food—it's never, ever boring. The difference between what ginger versus chipotle chiles brings to a dish is the difference between the sun and the moon. They're both miracles of nature to be discovered and explored.

THE MELLOWERS AND COOLERS
Yogurts. Cheeses. Nuts. Fresh fruits. Flowers. Herbs. Avocados. Creams. Butter.

All throughout India, Latin America, and Asia, where spicy foods are common, there is an interesting use of "cooling" foods as well. Often they come in the form of a dairy product used in combination: a yogurt raita sauce on top of a spicy curry, or a sour cream–like drizzle of crema over a chile relleno. You'll sometimes see the mellowing in the form of a cucumber salad served alongside a spicy meat satay, or a splash of mint chutney on a lentil fritter. Different cultures use these "mellowers" to help balance out the spice and cool a dish down. So if you're going to serve or taste anything hot, be sure to blend it with a "cooler," either on the plate or on the palate.

ABOUT CURRY
When I visited my friend Alan at the ashram in Ahmednagar, India, I found myself in the kitchen, or rather outside it, sitting on the floor of a tiny screened-in porch with a group of women. In a raised alcove on either side of a small fire, two of the women made chapatis: one woman rolled the dough, and the other cooked it off over the fire. Next to one of the women, her swaddled baby slept, lulled by the heat and their melodious laughter. With cinnamon skin, their arms loaded with multicolored bangle bracelets, many earrings in each ear, and their quick humor, these women became my heroines. As they laughed and baked and chatted, I learned.

What I learned is that curry is just a mixture of spices, not so complicated and nothing to be daunted by. Each area of the world has its own flavors and spice mixtures and its own ways to finish the curry. In some areas they finish it with coconut milk and lime, in others with tomato, vinegar, and brown sugar, but the basics are all the same. The mixture can be added to something like sweet potatoes to "curry" them, or you can actually make a stew.

To make a quick curry, caramelize onions, add garlic and ginger, cook your spices in the fat, and there's your curry base. Once a spice is ground it starts to lose its flavor, so buy whole seeds and toast them in a dry pan before grinding them in a spice grinder. You will be amazed at how taking a little bit of time to make your own curry blend, rather than buying a jar of curry powder at the store, will not only give you a much more flavorful end product but will also make you feel hugely accomplished.

RTERS & BITES

ARTICHOKES WITH LEMON ZA'ATAR DIPPING SAUCE 16

COCONUT CURRY CARAMEL CORN 18

UKRAINIAN SPINACH DUMPLINGS WITH LEMON MARMALADE AND SOUR CREAM 22

SALMON TARTARE WITH SPICY SESAME, CALIFORNIA AVOCADO, AND PINK PEPPERCORNS 26

SPICED MILLET PUFFS 27

MUNG BEAN PANCAKES WITH KOREAN PORK AND KIMCHI 28

MISO-GLAZED CHICKEN WINGS WITH GINGER SCALLION DIPPING SAUCE 31

TUNISIAN CHICKEN KEBABS WITH CURRANTS AND OLIVES 34

CANTONESE RADISH CAKES WITH CHINESE SAUSAGE 36

LAMB MEATBALLS WITH DATE AND CAROB MOLASSES 38

SHRIMP-STUFFED SHIITAKE MUSHROOMS 40

ARTICHOKES
WITH LEMON ZA'ATAR DIPPING SAUCE

3 large artichokes

1 lemon, quartered

2 tablespoons kosher salt

3 tablespoons extra virgin olive oil

Lemon Za'atar Dipping Sauce (recipe follows)

SERVES 6 If I had to pick one vegetable that was my absolute favorite, it would be the artichoke. Living in California, I'm spoiled because I actually grow them in my backyard. If I don't get around to picking all of them, they bloom into a gorgeous purple flower. I love to blanch artichokes as we do in this recipe, or to steam them and then finish them on the grill, brushed with olive oil and lemon. Sometimes I serve a second dipping sauce of mayonnaise, fresh lime, and lots of cracked black pepper.

Za'atar is the Arabic word for "thyme," but it is also used to describe a mixture of sesame seeds, dried thyme, and spices that is found all across the Middle East. This za'atar dipping sauce calls for sumac, an African spice that is also used in Middle Eastern cooking. The fruit of the sumac plant is a gorgeous deep red berry and, when it's ground, adds a lemony flavor to help balance the richness in a dish. If your local supermarket doesn't carry ground sumac, you can always find it in an Asian or Middle Eastern market.

1 To prepare the artichokes, first cut off the bottom portion of the stem, leaving only 1 inch of the stem attached. Using a sharp knife (sometimes a serrated knife works best for this), cut off the tip of the artichoke, slicing straight across about 2 inches down. Using scissors, clip off the sharp spikes on the tips of the remaining leaves.

2 Put the artichokes in a large pot, and add enough water to reach three-quarters of the way up the artichokes. Squeeze the lemon quarters into the water and then throw the quarters in as well. Add the salt and olive oil to the water. Cover, and cook over high heat until the water comes to a boil, about 15 minutes. Reduce the heat to low and simmer, still covered, for 30 minutes. Test an artichoke to see if it's done by gently tugging one of the lower leaves. It should come off easily but with resistance, and the whole leaf should pull out in one piece, not fall apart.

3 Turn off the heat. Remove the artichokes, put them upside down on a plate to drain, and let them cool to room temperature, 15 to 20 minutes.

4 Once they have cooled, cut each artichoke in half lengthwise. With a spoon, gently scoop out and discard the fuzzy inner choke and the pointy purple leaves that line the inside. Cut each half in half again, creating small portions that are more easily shared. Arrange them on a platter and serve with the lemon za'atar dipping sauce.

LEMON ZA'ATAR DIPPING SAUCE
MAKES 1¼ CUPS

1 cup mayonnaise

Juice of 1 lemon (about ¼ cup)

¼ cup sesame seeds, toasted

3 tablespoons dried thyme

2 teaspoons Dijon mustard

1 teaspoon ground sumac

1 teaspoon kosher salt

½ teaspoon cayenne pepper

Put the mayonnaise, lemon juice, sesame seeds, thyme, mustard, sumac, salt, and cayenne in a small mixing bowl. Stir well with a rubber spatula or a spoon to combine. The sauce can be refrigerated, with plastic wrap pressed against the surface, for up to 2 days.

COCONUT CURRY
CARAMEL CORN

Olive oil spray

1½ cups shredded unsweetened coconut

3 tablespoons canola oil

¾ cup popcorn kernels

2 cups Candied Peanuts (page 21)

1 cup (2 sticks) unsalted butter

2 cups packed dark brown sugar

½ cup light corn syrup

1½ teaspoons kosher salt

½ teaspoon baking soda

3 tablespoons chopped fresh curry leaf (see page 20; optional)

1 teaspoon cumin seeds

1 teaspoon black mustard seeds (see page 78)

1 teaspoon ground turmeric

½ teaspoon ground mace or nutmeg (optional)

½ teaspoon paprika

¼ teaspoon cayenne pepper (optional)

¼ teaspoon ground cinnamon

MAKES 18 CUPS This is the recipe to think about if you are going to a party—it would make a great gift instead of a bottle of wine. I recently prepared this as a party favor for a luncheon of 750 women, and they loved it. Even more noteworthy: I still loved it after making such a huge batch! That says a lot. The combination of sweet and spicy in the popcorn is what makes it different from anything else you've tasted.

1 Preheat the oven to 250°F. Liberally spray an extra-large mixing bowl (not plastic) with olive oil spray.

2 Spread the coconut on a baking sheet and toast it in the oven, stirring it once or twice, until it is golden, about 8 minutes. Set aside to cool, leaving the oven on.

3 Put the oil in a large heavy-bottomed pot, add the corn kernels, and set over medium-high heat. Cover, and shake the pot occasionally until the popping begins, about 5 minutes. Once the popping starts, shake the pot continuously until the popping slows down dramatically, 3 to 5 minutes. Remove the pot from the heat, but continue shaking it until the popping stops entirely. Dump the popcorn into the prepared mixing bowl, trying not to let any unpopped kernels fall into the bowl. Add the toasted coconut and the candied peanuts.

4 Before beginning the caramel process, spray a rubber spatula, a wooden spoon, and 2 cookie sheets liberally with olive oil spray.

5 In a medium saucepan, combine the butter, brown sugar, and corn syrup. Heat over medium-high heat, stirring occasionally with the oil-sprayed spatula, until the butter is melted. Continue cooking, stirring constantly and being careful not to splatter the hot caramel, until the mixture thickens and a candy thermometer registers 255°F, about

(recipe continues)

CURRY LEAF

Used in curries in India and Sri Lanka, curry leaf is fried along with chopped onion in the first stage of cooking. Usually called "curry leaves," they are also called "neem leaves" or "curry neem leaves." Curry leaf is what they call the "mystery ingredient" in India. Used everywhere but hard to describe, curry leaf has a slight nuttiness that adds backbone to the flavor of a dish. There really is no substitute, so if you can't find the leaves, simply omit them from the recipe.

7 minutes. (If you do not have a candy thermometer, you will know it is ready when the bubbles of the mixture get noticeably larger and slower.) Remove from the heat. Add the salt, baking soda, curry leaf, cumin seeds, black mustard seeds, turmeric, mace, paprika, cayenne, and cinnamon. Stir quickly to incorporate, and then immediately pour the caramel over the popcorn mixture. Stir with the wooden spoon until all of the popcorn is well coated.

6 Pour the mixture onto the oiled cookie sheets and spread it out evenly. Bake for 1 hour, stirring it every 20 minutes to keep it from burning.

7 Remove the cookie sheets from the oven and let the popcorn cool to room temperature. The popcorn will crisp as it cools.

8 When it is cool, you can serve the popcorn immediately or package it in airtight bags for storage. It will keep well for 4 days.

CANDIED PEANUTS MAKES 2 CUPS

2 cups unsalted peanuts

2 tablespoons well-shaken canned coconut milk

2 tablespoons packed dark brown sugar

1 tablespoon chopped fresh kaffir lime leaf (about 10 leaves)

½ teaspoon kosher salt

¼ teaspoon reshampatti chile powder or cayenne pepper (optional)

1 In a small mixing bowl, combine the peanuts, coconut milk, brown sugar, kaffir lime leaf, salt, and reshampatti. Put the mixture in a nonstick sauté pan and cook over high heat without stirring until the nuts have started to brown and toast, about 2 minutes. Then stir, and continue to cook, stirring, for 5 minutes or until the peanuts have browned. (The nuts will brown unevenly and the pan may smoke slightly from the coconut milk, but this is all okay if you are stirring continuously.)

2 Transfer the mixture to a plate and set aside to cool. The nuts will still be somewhat moist at this point but will crisp as they cool.

3 Once the nuts are cool, break them up. Store in an airtight container at room temperature.

KAFFIR LIME LEAF

A thorny bush with aromatic, hourglass-shaped leaves, common to Southeast Asia, kaffir lime has an intense and unique pepper-lime flavor. It is also called "kieffer lime," "makrut," or "magrood." If you can't find it, you can substitute grated lime zest.

UKRAINIAN SPINACH DUMPLINGS
WITH LEMON MARMALADE AND SOUR CREAM

DOUGH

1 large egg, beaten

⅓ cup sour cream

3¼ cups all-purpose flour, plus more for rolling

1 teaspoon kosher salt

8 tablespoons (1 stick) cold unsalted butter, cut into small pieces

FILLING

2 Yukon Gold potatoes, peeled and cut into 8 equal pieces

2 teaspoons kosher salt

2½ tablespoons olive oil

1 white onion, cut into small dice

2½ pounds zucchini, grated (4 cups)

2 bunches fresh spinach, roughly chopped (8 cups)

5 ounces feta cheese, crumbled (1 cup)

6 tablespoons (¾ stick) unsalted butter

1 cup sour cream

1 cup Lemon Marmalade (page 153)

¼ cup chopped fresh dill, for garnish

SERVES 4 TO 6 All throughout Eastern Europe you see versions of this type of dumpling. Often they are filled with fruit, which is what inspired the lemon marmalade I use here. In Russian, these are called *varenyky,* which means "little boiled thing." The blending of tangy feta cheese, the earthiness of the spinach, and that sweet layer of lemon marmalade makes this dish a favorite at STREET.

1 Make the dough: In a small bowl, mix the egg and sour cream together.

2 Put the flour and the salt in the bowl of a stand mixer fitted with the paddle attachment. With the mixer on low speed, beat the mixture while adding the butter, one piece at a time, until the flour starts to come together in small clumps, about 2 minutes. Stop the mixer and add the egg mixture all at once. Turn the mixer on low speed again, and mix just enough to incorporate the egg mixture. Do not overmix or your dough will be tough. The consistency will be slightly crumbly and will resemble a pie dough.

3 Turn the dough out onto a flat surface. Knead it with your hands just enough to bring the dough together into a ball. Wrap it in plastic wrap and refrigerate it for at least 1 hour or for as long as 24 hours.

4 Divide the dough in half. Put one half on a floured work surface; wrap the other half in plastic wrap and return it to the refrigerator. Roll the dough out into a round about ⅛ inch thick. Cut out 12 rounds with a 3-inch cookie cutter. Put the rounds on a plate, cover with plastic wrap, and refrigerate until ready to use. Repeat with the other half of the dough to make 24 rounds total.

5 Make the filling: Put the potatoes and 1 teaspoon of the salt in a small saucepan, cover with water, and set

over high heat. Bring to a boil. Then reduce the heat to medium-low and continue to cook at a slow boil for 15 minutes, or until the potatoes are very tender when poked with a fork. Drain, and set aside until cool enough to handle, 5 to 10 minutes.

6 While the potatoes are cooking, heat the olive oil in a large sauté pan set over medium-high heat. Add the onion and cook, stirring frequently, until it is translucent and just beginning to brown, 3 to 4 minutes. Add the zucchini and ¼ teaspoon of the salt. Cook, stirring constantly, for 2 minutes. The onion will continue to brown; that is okay. Add the spinach and ¼ teaspoon of the salt. Cook, stirring, for 2 minutes.

7 Remove the pan from the heat and pour the entire contents into a colander, pushing on them slightly to expel some of the liquid. Let drain and cool in the colander for 30 minutes, occasionally pressing and stirring with a rubber spatula to drain as much of the excess liquid as possible.

8 Grate the potatoes on the large holes of a box grater.

9 When the drained spinach mixture is cool, put it in a large mixing bowl. Add the grated potato, feta cheese, and the last ½ teaspoon salt. Mix gently to combine.

(recipe continues)

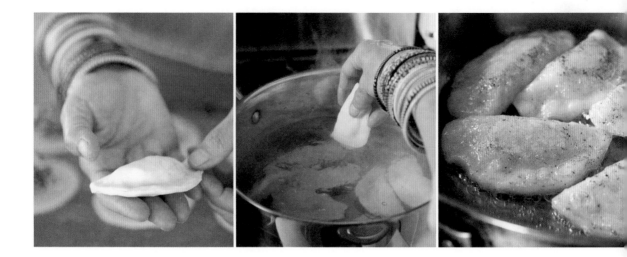

10 Make the dumplings: Put a large pot of water on the stove to boil.

11 Put a level tablespoon of the filling in the center of each dough round. Fold the dough into a half-moon shape, and making sure the filling doesn't squeeze out, press the edges together firmly with your fingers to seal them. The dough is pliable, so if there seems to be too much filling, you can stretch it a little bit to fit around it. Repeat until all of the dumplings are filled.

12 Working in batches, boil the dumplings for 3 minutes and then drain them, being careful that they don't tear. Set them aside on a tray lined with wax paper. (The dumplings can be covered and refrigerated for up to 1 day at this point.)

13 Melt the butter in a large sauté pan over medium-high heat. When the butter is frothy, add the dumplings so that they lie in a single layer. (You may have to do this in two or three batches, depending on the size of your pan.) Cook for just 1 to 2 minutes on each side, until they have a light golden brown sear and are slightly crispy but are not fully browned or fried.

14 To serve, spread a generous spoonful of sour cream across the center of each plate. Follow with a spoonful of the lemon marmalade. Put the dumplings on top, and sprinkle with the dill.

SALMON TARTARE
WITH SPICY SESAME, CALIFORNIA AVOCADO, AND PINK PEPPERCORNS

3 tablespoons Japanese mayonnaise (see page 108)

1½ tablespoons spicy sesame oil

2 tablespoons yuzu juice (see page 154)

1½ teaspoons kosher salt

1 pound wild salmon fillet, cut into ¼-inch dice

2 ripe Hass avocados, diced

2 to 3 small shallots, minced

1 (1-inch) piece fresh ginger, peeled and minced

2 tablespoons chopped fresh chives

1 teaspoon crushed pink peppercorns

Fresh radish sprouts, for garnish (optional)

Rice crackers, for serving

SERVES 4 TO 6 People are often afraid of making tartare at home, but it's so easy. There's no cooking involved, so that cuts out one big step. The key here is to dice all the fish the same size. The pink peppercorns add sweetness, the avocado richness, and the sesame oil a toasted earthiness. When you taste something that is too rich, consider adding acid—such as the yuzu juice here. It typically takes the dish to another level, right where you want it.

1 To make the dressing, in a large bowl, combine the mayonnaise, sesame oil, yuzu juice, and salt. Whisk well to blend.

2 In a separate bowl, combine the fish, avocados, shallots, ginger, chives, and pink peppercorns. Pour the dressing over the fish and mix well but gently to incorporate all of the ingredients. The tartare is ready to eat immediately, but it can be held for up to 4 hours, covered, in the refrigerator.

3 To serve, divide the tartare among 4 to 6 bowls and lay the radish sprouts over the top for garnish. Pass the rice crackers.

SUSTAINABLE SEAFOOD Many species of fish have been overfished around the world, and consequently their populations have been decimated. On top of that, natural habitats have been destroyed and our oceans polluted in the process. Think of our oceans as being the canary in the coal mine: As the oceans go, so goes the world. We are the stewards, so it's critical to protect the integrity and health of the water that covers three-fourths of the planet! The Monterey Bay Aquarium has developed guidelines for purchasing seafood, aimed at ensuring that the species we enjoy today will still be around for our grandchildren. You can look online to learn more: www.montereybayaquarium.org.

SPICED MILLET PUFFS

MAKES 70 MINI PUFFS On the streets of India and elsewhere in Asia, chaat stands are everywhere, serving small savory bites of all different types of snacks. Some of these snacks are puffed grains, like rice or millet, tossed with a spiced mixture. The scents that fill the air make walking around an amazing treat for your nose! This spiced millet puff is the first bite of food that people taste when they arrive at STREET, and it's always a conversation starter.

1 In a large skillet or shallow saucepan, heat the butter over medium heat until it is frothy, 3 to 4 minutes. Add the marshmallows and start to melt them, pushing and stirring them with a rubber spatula so they don't burn on the bottom of the pan. (You can lower the heat slightly if you need to.)

2 When the marshmallows are halfway melted, add the dried currants, cumin seeds, fennel seeds, black mustard seeds, curry leaf, turmeric, cayenne, and salt, and stir well so that the spices toast and mix with the marshmallows. Add the millet, remove from the heat, and stir until all of the millet is mixed in and evenly coated with the spiced marshmallow mixture. Pour the mixture out into a bowl.

3 Immediately start rolling the mixture into very small balls. (If you find that the mixture is sticking to your hands too much, dampen your hands slightly with cold water.) Put the balls in a bowl and serve immediately. They can also be stored in an airtight container at room temperature for up to 2 days.

2 tablespoons unsalted butter

1 (5-ounce) bag mini marshmallows (3 cups)

½ cup dried currants or black raisins

1 tablespoon cumin seeds

1 teaspoon fennel seeds

1 teaspoon black mustard seeds (see page 78)

1 teaspoon chopped fresh curry leaf (see page 20; optional)

¼ teaspoon ground turmeric

¼ teaspoon cayenne pepper

½ teaspoon kosher salt

3 cups puffed millet

PUFFED MILLET

An all-natural, air-puffed millet cereal that is readily available in the United States. I use Arrowhead Mills brand.

MUNG BEAN PANCAKES
WITH KOREAN PORK AND KIMCHI

1 cup dried mung bean dal (see page 30)

½ pound boneless pork shoulder, cut into ½-inch cubes

1 cup Five-Spice Marinade (page 161)

1 teaspoon kosher salt

2 tablespoons canola oil

1 bunch scallions, green and white parts, cut into 2-inch pieces

1 cup kimchi, roughly chopped

Chinese hot mustard or other spicy mustard, for serving (optional)

Soy sauce, for serving (optional)

KIMCHI

Pickled fermented vegetables, brined in garlic, Korean chile, and spices, are a staple in the Korean kitchen.

There are hundreds of varieties, often including preserved fish or dried shrimp.

SERVES 4 TO 6 All over the world, people leave dried beans soaking in water for a day or two so that they begin to ferment and take on a lightness from the natural yeast that forms. They then grind them up to make a batter or dough that is slightly tangy and indescribably airy. It's a simple technique that gives wonderful flavor to dishes. While I use mung beans here, you can ferment many different kinds of beans (most often the dal, or inner part, of the beans is used). If you want to make this recipe vegan, omit the pork and add any great vegetable, such as lotus root or roasted carrots.

For the best results, start this recipe two days in advance. The beans will need time to ferment and the ground batter will need time to rise.

1 Rinse and drain the mung bean dal, put it in a large container, and add 5 cups warm water. Cover and let sit in a warm place (next to a stove or in an oven area) overnight.

2 Put the pork and five-spice marinade in a bowl and mix well to combine. Cover with plastic wrap, put in the refrigerator, and let marinate overnight.

3 The next day, drain the beans and put them in a food processor. Add the salt. Puree until smooth, adding fresh water as you go to thin the mix into a thin pancake-batter consistency (you'll use about ¾ cup water). You may need to do this in batches, depending on the size of your food processor. Pour the batter into a container, cover with plastic wrap, and leave it in a warm place for at least 4 hours (overnight is ideal). The batter should remain thin. If it thickens while sitting, stir in a little bit more water before using.

(recipe continues)

MUNG BEAN DAL

Found throughout Asia, Southeast Asia, India, and Pakistan, dals are legumes that have been stripped of their outer hulls and split. They are cooked in a similar fashion to whole legumes, but they cook much more quickly. Mung bean dal is from the mung bean.

4 Heat the oil in a large sauté pan or skillet over medium-low heat. Pull the pork out of its marinade and put the pork in the pan. Cook, stirring occasionally, until it is browned and crispy on the outside but still soft when pressed, about 10 minutes. Pour the excess fat and oil out of the pan and discard. Raise the heat to medium and put the pan back on the stove. Add the scallions and sauté for 2 minutes, or until they are wilted and starting to brown. Add the chopped kimchi, stir well, and remove from the heat. Pour the mixture into a bowl.

5 Heat a small nonstick pan over medium heat. Pour about ½ cup of the batter into the center. Your batter should be fairly thin and should spread out on its own to create a 4-inch pancake. While the pancake is cooking on the first side, sprinkle 3 tablespoons of the pork mixture on the pancake, being sure that it is equally distributed over the surface. After about 3 minutes, when the pancake is starting to brown and the edges to crisp, flip it over with a spatula and press down slightly to push the pork mixture into the pancake. Cook for 2 to 3 minutes. Then transfer the pancake to a platter, pork side up. Continue making pancakes with the remaining ingredients.

6 Serve the pancakes hot on their own, or with Chinese hot mustard and soy sauce.

MISO-GLAZED CHICKEN WINGS
WITH GINGER SCALLION DIPPING SAUCE

SERVES 4 TO 6 When frying chicken wings, use a shallow pan—it's much more manageable than a deep pan. Make sure the pan is hot so the wings get crisp, and then, after frying, immediately dip them into the miso glaze. When the wings are hot, they absorb the sweet and earthy flavors of the glaze much more than if they are at room temperature. You can make the glaze up to 4 days in advance and store it in the refrigerator.

1 Put the oven rack in the top third of the oven, and preheat the oven to 400°F.

2 In a medium bowl, combine the chicken wings, scallions, ginger, sesame oil, and salt. Toss gently until the wings are coated evenly with the scallions and ginger. Spread the wings out, skin side up, in a single layer on a nonstick cookie sheet.

3 Bake in the oven for 20 minutes. Then rotate the cookie sheet 180 degrees and bake for 15 minutes, or until the wings are starting to brown slightly and are cooked through. Remove from the oven and let cool at room temperature for 15 to 20 minutes, until only slightly warm to the touch.

4 Meanwhile, heat the canola oil in a deep saucepan set over medium heat for about 5 minutes, or until you hear the oil start to crackle slightly and a deep-frying thermometer registers 350°F. Do not let the oil smoke; that will mean the temperature is too high. Set a baking sheet lined with paper towels near the saucepan.

5 Working with about 10 chicken wings at a time, carefully drop the wings into the oil and cook for about 6 minutes, until they are crispy and browned. While they are cooking,

(recipe continues)

2½ pounds chicken wings (preferably center cut), drumsticks and tips removed

4 scallions, white and green parts, finely chopped

1 (2-inch) piece fresh ginger, peeled and minced (about 3 tablespoons)

2 tablespoons spicy sesame oil

1½ tablespoons kosher salt

3 to 4 cups canola oil, for frying

1½ cups Korean Miso Barbecue Glaze (page 156)

1 cup Ginger Scallion Dipping Sauce (page 159)

lightly stir the wings occasionally so they don't stick to the bottom of the pan or to one another. Remove them from the oil with a slotted spoon or a strainer, and drop them onto the paper-towel-lined baking sheet. Let the oil reheat for 2 minutes before cooking the next batch of wings. Repeat the process until all of the chicken wings are cooked.

6 If you have made the miso glaze in advance, reheat it in a small saucepan for 3 to 4 minutes, until the sauce is warmed through.

7 Transfer the miso glaze to a medium bowl, add the fried chicken wings, and toss thoroughly until the wings are well coated. Serve with the ginger scallion dipping sauce.

TUNISIAN CHICKEN KEBABS
WITH CURRANTS AND OLIVES

½ cup dried currants

4 ounces (1 cup) jarred Peppadew peppers, plus ¼ cup of their juice

1 large red bell pepper, roasted, peeled, and seeded

½ cup extra virgin olive oil

Kosher salt

2 pounds boneless, skinless chicken breasts, cut into 1-inch cubes

Tunisian Relish (recipe follows)

PEPPADEW PEPPERS

These sweet piquant peppers (*Capsicum baccatum*) are grown in the Limpopo province of South Africa. Available in cans or jars, they can be found in specialty grocery stores. If you can't find them, any sweet pickled pepper could work.

SERVES 4 Chicken breast meat will dry out very quickly, so be sure not to overcook it. The robust combination of marinade and relish in this recipe makes the mild-flavored chicken sing. It's perfect served warm or at room temperature.

1 Put the currants in a bowl and add ¼ cup warm water. Let sit until the currants have plumped, about 10 minutes.

2 Drain the currants and put them in a blender. Add the Peppadews, their juice, the bell pepper, oil, and 1 tablespoon salt, and puree on high speed until smooth. Pour half of this mixture into a bowl, add the chicken, and mix well. Cover and refrigerate for at least 30 minutes, or up to 4 hours. Save the remaining puree for a later use.

3 Heat a grill or griddle to high.

4 Slide 4 to 6 cubes of chicken on each of about 8 skewers. Salt the chicken to taste, and then grill, turning the skewers so that the chicken browns on all sides, 5 minutes total. Remove from the grill, brush with the reserved puree, and top each skewer with a spoonful of the relish.

TUNISIAN RELISH   MAKES 1½ CUPS

½ cup dried currants or black raisins

1 cup pitted green olives (such as Manzanilla), chopped

½ cup Peppadew peppers, finely chopped

¼ cup extra virgin olive oil

¼ cup aged sherry vinegar

½ teaspoon kosher salt

1 Put the currants in a bowl and add warm water to cover. Let sit until the currants have plumped, about 10 minutes.

2 Drain, discarding the water, and put the currants into a bowl. Add the olives, Peppadews, oil, vinegar, and salt. Stir well to combine, and serve. You can make the relish up to 2 days in advance and store it, covered, in the refrigerator. Bring it to room temperature and stir it before serving.

CANTONESE RADISH CAKES
WITH CHINESE SAUSAGE

2 cups jasmine rice

2 teaspoons kosher salt

4 tablespoons canola oil

4 Chinese sausages, cut into small cubes

1 white onion, diced

2 tablespoons dried shrimp, rinsed and chopped (optional)

4 cups packed grated daikon radish (see opposite)

Soy sauce, Chinese mustard, or Green Sriracha Sauce (see page 157), for serving

DRIED SHRIMP

Used frequently in Southeast Asia for their salty flavor, the shrimp are soaked in a salted solution for curing and then sun-dried, causing them to shrink. Dried shrimp have the unusual *umami* ("fifth taste") flavor.

MAKES 1 (9 × 4-INCH) LOAF CAKE; SERVES 12

This is a typical Chinese dim sum dish, but most people have never tasted anything like it. The recipe came directly from Kajsa, the executive chef and my partner at STREET, who ate this dish as a kid. Her mom, who is Cantonese and grew up in the heart of New York City's Chinatown, says the rice dough represents your fortune: as it cooks and rises, your fortune grows. Being chefs, we tweaked it a bit, and being a chef's mom, she still insists her version is better! The texture is loaflike and easy to slice, which makes it perfect for browning in hot oil. The sweetness of the Chinese sausage and the texture of the cake make it an ideal bed for a fried egg. You'll need to start the rice for this recipe early in the morning or in the evening before baking. This cake is most delicious when made a day or two before serving.

1 Put the rice in a medium mixing bowl and rinse it under running water, stirring it with your hand to release some of the starch. Drain, and then pour 4 cups warm water over the rice. Cover the bowl with plastic wrap and let the rice soak for a minimum of 6 hours or as long as overnight at room temperature.

2 Drape a 9 × 4-inch loaf pan with long sheets of plastic wrap that generously hang over all four sides.

3 Set a steaming rack into a roasting pan or wide saucepan, and add 3 inches of water. Make sure to use a pan that is large enough to hold the loaf pan.

4 Drain the rice (do not rinse it), and combine it in a food processor with 1 cup cold water and the salt. Process for 3 to 5 minutes, until smooth.

5 In a medium sauté pan, heat 2 tablespoons of the oil over medium-high heat. Add the sausages and onion and cook, stirring occasionally, until the onion is soft and translucent

and just starting to color, about 5 minutes. Add the dried shrimp, if using, and cook for a minute or two. Remove from the heat and transfer to a large mixing bowl.

6   Add the daikon radish and the ground rice mixture, and stir so that all of the ingredients are well combined and the sausages and onion are evenly distributed throughout the mixture. Scoop into the loaf pan and tap the pan on the counter to force out any air bubbles. Fold the excess plastic wrap over the top.

7   Set the loaf pan inside your prepared steaming pan, and cover the steaming pan with a lid or tightly fitting aluminum foil. Set the pan over low heat and steam for 1 hour, checking the water level after 30 minutes. Turn off the heat and carefully lift the lid, avoiding the hot steam. Remove the loaf pan and let it cool to room temperature. Then let it cool completely in the refrigerator, at least 3 hours or up to overnight.

8   Remove the cake from the pan by lifting out the plastic wrap. Put it on a cutting board, unwrap and discard the plastic wrap. Cut the loaf into ½-inch-thick slices, and then cut each slice in half. The cakes can be stored at this stage in an airtight container in the refrigerator for up to 4 days.

9   To serve, heat a nonstick skillet over medium heat. Add the remaining 2 tablespoons oil, and sear the radish cakes until they are golden brown, 2 to 3 minutes on each side. Serve with soy sauce, Chinese mustard, or Sriracha chile sauce.

DAIKON RADISH

A winter vegetable with a mild flavor, resembling a giant white carrot, daikon is also called "Chinese radish," "lo bok," and sometimes even "carrot" in Asian markets. But it is very large and white, not orange like a carrot, and found in most well-stocked grocery stores, so do not fear!

5 tablespoons canola oil

1 large white onion, diced (about 3 cups)

4 cloves garlic, chopped

1 pound ground lamb

1 bunch fresh Italian parsley, chopped (about ¾ cup)

1½ teaspoons paprika

¼ teaspoon cayenne pepper (optional)

1 teaspoon kosher salt

¼ teaspoon freshly ground black pepper

3 tablespoons date molasses (optional)

2 tablespoons carob molasses (optional)

12 pitted dates, fresh or dried, cut in half lengthwise

DATE AND CAROB "MOLASSES"

Found in Middle Eastern markets, these are actually thick syrups that are made with pressed fruit and are sometimes smoked with Arabian incense. If they're not available, pomegranate molasses—which is easier to find—can be used in their place.

MAKES 24 MEATBALLS In the United States, we don't usually see ground meat on skewers, but it is typical throughout the Middle East and Africa. The trick to this dish is not to overmix the lamb, so it doesn't become mealy. I like these meatballs nice and small so the bite you get is fully caramelized—lamb on the outside, onion on the inside.

1 Heat a large sauté pan over medium heat. Add 3 tablespoons of the oil and the onion, and cook, stirring occasionally, until the onion is transparent, 5 to 7 minutes. Reduce the heat to low and add the garlic. Cook for 5 minutes, or just before the garlic starts to brown. Remove the pan from the heat and let cool to room temperature.

2 In a large bowl, combine the cooled onion mixture with the lamb, parsley, paprika, cayenne, salt, and black pepper. Mix well with your hands to combine all the ingredients thoroughly, but be sure not to overmix or the meatballs will be tough. Scoop up 2 tablespoons of the meat mixture, roll it into a ball, and put it on a baking sheet or plate. Repeat to make 24 meatballs.

3 Heat a large sauté pan over medium heat. Add the remaining 2 tablespoons oil to the pan, and then, working in batches, add the meatballs carefully so as not to splatter the hot oil. Sear the meatballs for 3 minutes, or until they start to brown. Continue to brown the meatballs, rolling them to cook all sides, until they are browned all the way around, about 10 minutes total. Remove the pan from the heat.

4 To serve, drizzle the meatballs with the date molasses and the carob molasses, if using. Run a toothpick or a small skewer through the center of each date half and then through the center of each meatball. Serve on a platter.

SHRIMP-STUFFED
SHIITAKE MUSHROOMS

8 ounces shrimp, peeled, deveined, and tails removed

5 fresh shiso leaves (see opposite)

2 tablespoons minced peeled fresh ginger

2 teaspoons kosher salt

5 ounces fresh shiitake mushrooms (20 to 25 mushrooms), stemmed

2 cups all-purpose flour

1½ cups sparkling water

3 cups canola oil, for frying

1 cup ponzu sauce or soy sauce mixed with lemon juice, for dipping

MAKES 20 TO 25 MUSHROOMS One of our sous chefs, Christine Brashear, used to eat a dish similar to this one when she was a child. Her mother, who was Japanese, would whip these up as an afternoon snack. When she told me about it, I loved the idea, and with a few tweaks, here is my version.

There are a few tricks for perfect deep-frying. First, when you flour something before battering, make sure that you pat off any excess flour. A clump of flour will fall free as soon as you drop the food into the batter, creating a spot without any batter. No batter means oil gets in and makes your food greasy. And second, if the oil isn't hot enough, even if you've floured and battered perfectly, oil will seep in because the batter won't seal first. Even if your end result is crispy, it will be greasy. To test the oil to see if it's hot, drop a tiny piece of batter into the oil. If it doesn't sink and instantly floats to the top, you're ready to go.

1 In a food processor, combine the shrimp, shiso, ginger, and 1 teaspoon of the salt. Pulse until the mixture is smooth. (Do not run the blade continuously or the shrimp will become tough when cooked.)

2 Put 1 heaping teaspoon of the shrimp mixture inside each mushroom cap and press down on the filling so it is packed tightly inside and slightly mounded.

3 In a medium mixing bowl, combine 1 cup of the flour with the remaining 1 teaspoon salt. Slowly whisk in the sparkling water until the mixture forms a smooth batter.

4 Pour the canola oil into a deep, heavy-bottomed pot or cast-iron skillet. Make sure that there is plenty of space (at least 3 inches) at the top of the pot for the oil to expand as it heats. Heat the oil over medium heat for 4 to 5 minutes, or until a drop of batter floats immediately and a deep-frying thermometer registers 350°F.

5 Put the remaining 1 cup flour in a small bowl. Working in batches, dredge each of the stuffed mushrooms in the flour so they are completely coated, and then tap off any excess. Dip the mushrooms into the batter, and with a spoon, turn them over in the batter until they are completely covered.

6 Carefully drop a few of the mushrooms into the hot oil and push them down with a slotted spoon to keep them submerged in the oil. (The mushrooms have a tendency to float.) Cook for 2 to 3 minutes, or until golden brown. Remove from the oil with the slotted spoon, and drain on a paper towel. Repeat until you have fried all the mushrooms.

7 Serve with the ponzu sauce, or soy sauce with lemon, alongside for dipping.

SHISO LEAF

A Japanese herb that is also used in Vietnam, shiso, or perilla, has somewhat round and spiky leaves. It can be either purple or green and has a distinctive aromatic flavor, somewhere between mint and basil. It can be found in most Asian markets and well-stocked grocery stores.

HO CHI MINH CITY, VIETNAM

Throw your dreams into space like a kite, and you do not know what it will bring back, a new life, a new friend, a new love, a new country. —ANAÏS NIN

"Oh, oh, oh, ohhh. I love you more than I can say, oh." This is the song Captain Cook keeps singing over and over as we sit in a van (or as I like to call it, a "heat-seeking missile") in a traffic jam in Ho Chi Minh City, Vietnam. Captain Cook (his real name is Ha Vanchau)—the guide I hired on the recommendation of my friend back in Los Angeles, chef Robert Danhi, an Asian food expert—has picked me up for a full day of eating in the former Saigon.

There are 10 million inhabitants and 7 million two-wheeled vehicles in this city, and along every main thoroughfare hang huge red banners with a yellow sickle and star—the Communist flag. The streets are absolutely clogged with bicycles, motorcycles, motorized bicycles—it's bedlam. Everyone rides, from grannies to young folks, from men with little kids balanced in front of them to women with their dogs in a basket on the front of their motorbikes. And all of them, except the dogs, wear bandannas to cover their faces, which makes me wonder if I somehow missed the memo about not breathing the air. The constant barrage of cycles beeping and cutting in and out of traffic has me on edge, but Captain is doing his best to distract me. He's one of

the most gregarious people I've ever met: a cook, a war hero, and a real comedian. He constantly stops in the middle of a sentence to pose and flex his biceps. Now he insists the song he's singing was a huge hit all over Vietnam in the 1980s, came from America, and surely I must have heard it. When I shake my head no it only encourages another verse, as if hearing it yet another time will suddenly jog my memory.

The first place we hit is the Cho Lon Market. It's a huge covered market with alleys and lanes shooting out in every direction, and when we walk in, my senses are bombarded with all of the colors, scents, and people. Captain takes me to a stand offering sugarcane juice. The vendor puts long, reedy shoots of raw sugarcane into a press, and out comes the juice. It's wonderfully refreshing in the incredible heat and stifling humidity of the monsoon season. While I sip my sugarcane juice, I get my bearings before Captain shepherds me to another stand.

This next stand is all kimchi. A Korean woman and her two daughters sell some of the best pickled vegetables and sauerkraut I've ever tasted, with colors ranging from white to pink to dark red to

green, depending on which kind of chiles she used in the recipe. I try a pickled daikon radish that is really sour and wonderful. Captain says something to her in Vietnamese, and she tosses some batter on a hot cooking plate to make a pancake. As the pancake cooks, she puts a mixture of kimchi on the top and then flips it over, cooking both sides. They laugh and talk as she pulls it off the heat, cuts it, pours hot mustard over it, and hands it to me. I think I may be in heaven. My favorite flavors of sour, hot, and a little sweet from the rice vinegar in the kimchi all blend perfectly.

Now I'm walking down an aisle lined with huge barrels of different kinds of dried shrimp in all forms—ground,

ground rough, fermented as paste. When I get to the meat, fish, and produce alley, most of it looks familiar, although I must admit I'm not used to seeing seafood still alive. And definitely the most disconcerting thing is a bowl full of frogs, skinned and headless . . . and still alive. I'm immediately aware of the differences in our cultures and take a deep breath. Captain steers me to a dragon fruit stand, with huge green fruits sprouting red horns or spines, reminiscent of a dragon's back. Inside, the gorgeous flesh of the fruit is white with tiny dark seeds. It has a peculiar mild flavor, almost like a kiwi mixed with a melon. Outside the busy market, a woman sells longan fruit out of a huge basket on her bicycle. Captain

peels one of the small brown berries for me to taste, and I find that it's very similar to lychee nut, but sweeter.

Crossing the street in this city is a harrowing experience. There is no letting up of the thousands of bicycles and motorbikes going by, so the only way to do it is to simply walk out into the middle of the traffic, which is absolutely counterintuitive. Captain says: "Whatever you do, don't stop. They will go around you, but if you stop you'll get hit." So we wade into the street, never stopping, and amazingly they do go around us. After all the excitement of the market and just getting across the street, Captain senses that I need a little break so he takes me to a small stand where I have my first taste of *café sua da.* This is the famous dark-

roasted Vietnamese coffee dripped over sweetened condensed milk, which makes a beautiful black and white drink until you stir it all together and pour it over crushed ice. In the 100° heat, we sit on low plastic stools a few inches off the ground, at tiny plastic tables, and sip this sweet bit of heaven. There are lines and lines of motorbikes parked in rows on the street, and right now I'm sitting with my head next to a tire—but I don't care because I have discovered this new amazing drink.

Next up is *bun thit nuong.* Captain takes me to a street stand where there is a huge ten-foot-long grill loaded with pork skewers. There is one guy tending the grill and one replenishing the wood burning underneath. A woman at a stand behind them makes up bowls of *bun thit nuong*: skewers of grilled pork over rice noodles with shredded braised pork, cucumbers, carrots, chopped cilantro, peanuts, mixed lettuces, and lots of herbs, including Thai basil. She serves the dish with a side sauce to be poured over it, a combination of fish sauce, chiles, garlic, lime, and sugar. This *nuoc cham* is a sauce that's served as a condiment all over the country. *Bun thit nuong* is one of the most amazing dishes I've ever tasted. Captain tells the woman I'm a chef from America and she starts to show me all that she's doing, answering my millions of questions, all translated through Captain. Even though we don't speak the same language, once I show an interest, we end up laughing and bonding over food. Hilariously, she uses scissors to cut the egg rolls in half. What a great idea! The best part is that we go into the alley to eat. I sit here eating this fantastic dish, completely oblivious to the fact that I'm seven inches off the ground, in an alley between two buildings, and every few seconds a motorbike goes whizzing by with a high nasal *beep*. That's *some* good food.

For dinner we head over to a different part of Ho Chi Minh City where, according to Captain, we will taste some of the best *banh xeo* (translated as "sizzle crepes" for the sound they make while cooking) in the city. There are three cooks, each sitting on a low stool right off the sidewalk, in front of open cook fires, handling five fires each.

They're in constant motion, since each pan is in a different part of the cooking process. The cooks pour a thin crepe batter made of rice flour, coconut milk, and turmeric into a pan of oil and pat it flat while it cooks. They top it with pork, shrimp, and bean sprouts and flip it over like an omelet. The vendors coordinate all of this at lightning speed, constantly moving the pans from one cook fire to the next. It's a real art, and they are every bit as good as any busy line cook in any of the fancy kitchens where I've worked.

The alley is jam-packed, everyone sitting at long communal tables waiting for *banh xeo.* When we get ours, I load the top with mint, shiso (also called perilla), and Thai basil, then roll it up and dip it in *nuoc cham*. It is fantastic! So here I sit: at a picnic table, in an alley off a city street, the only Caucasian in sight. Somewhere a guitar and tambourine serenade the diners as a group of people clink their beer cans together and yell "Yo!" (their version of "Cheers!"). And then Captain starts to sing again: "Oh, oh, oh, ohhh. I love you more than I can say, oh." He grins and flexes his bicep yet again, and I laugh, oddly content in this strange new world.

That song drove me so crazy that I finally looked it up once I was back in the States. It was a Leo Sayer hit from 1980 called (what else?) "More Than I Can Say." Captain's version, as mangled and bastardized as it was, is now the only version of that song that I can sing. *Yo!*

S

SALADS

HEIRLOOM TOMATOES WITH BLACK GARLIC AND BASIL VINAIGRETTE 48

MOROCCAN CARROT SALAD WITH HARISSA VINAIGRETTE 49

KOREAN CHOPPED SALAD WITH SESAME DRESSING 50

SCANDINAVIAN MIXED GREENS AND APPLES WITH JUNIPER VINAIGRETTE 53

BABY BEET SALAD WITH KUMQUAT, MINT, AND CORIANDER 55

BURMESE *GIN THOKE* MELON SALAD 56

OLIVE BREAD FATTOUSH WITH JERUSALEM ARTICHOKES 59

SAIGON CHICKEN SALAD 60

INDIAN PUFFED RICE SALAD 62

HEIRLOOM TOMATOES
WITH BLACK GARLIC AND BASIL VINAIGRETTE

2 pounds assorted heirloom tomatoes, cored and cut into small wedges

Leaves from 1 bunch fresh basil, chopped (⅓ cup)

Kosher salt

½ cup black garlic cloves

⅓ cup balsamic vinegar

⅓ cup extra virgin olive oil

1 tablespoon honey

SERVES 4 TO 6 If you don't have access to heirloom tomatoes for this recipe, use any delicious ones you can find. This vinaigrette is also perfect as a marinade over any vegetable, like blanched green beans or roasted cauliflower, or as a barbecue sauce, or even mixed with mayonnaise as a spread for sandwiches.

1 Put the tomatoes and basil in a large mixing bowl. Season with salt to taste, and mix well to combine.

2 In a blender, combine the black garlic cloves, balsamic vinegar, olive oil, honey, and 1 teaspoon kosher salt. Puree until smooth. The mixture will be slightly thick.

3 Pour half of the vinaigrette over the tomatoes and mix well to combine. Serve the remaining vinaigrette on the side, or save it for a later use.

BLACK GARLIC

Made by fermenting whole bulbs of garlic at high temperatures, a process that results in black cloves, black garlic—common in Asia—has a taste that is mild, sweet, and syrupy, with hints of balsamic vinegar. If you can't find black garlic, you can roast a whole head of garlic in the oven until soft and then puree it with the balsamic vinegar in this recipe.

MOROCCAN CARROT SALAD
WITH HARISSA VINAIGRETTE

SERVES 4 TO 6 Throughout this book you'll see that many of the salad dressings start with a basic vinaigrette. To that I add ingredients like spices, cheese, fresh herbs, even something sweet like maple syrup. In this recipe I spruce up a basic lemon vinaigrette with chile sauce, parsley, and feta cheese.

1 In a medium mixing bowl, combine the carrots, raisins, parsley, and feta cheese. Toss gently.

2 In a separate bowl, whisk together the harissa, lemon juice, olive oil, and salt until well blended. Pour the harissa dressing over the carrot mixture, and stir well to evenly coat all the ingredients. Serve immediately.

HARISSA

 A fiery Tunisian hot chile sauce typically composed of bird's-eye chile peppers, serrano peppers, and other hot chiles, harissa is often mixed with garlic paste, coriander, caraway, and olive oil. You can substitute Sriracha sauce, which many grocery stores now carry.

3 jumbo carrots, peeled and julienned (about 6 cups)

1 cup black raisins

2 cups fresh Italian parsley leaves

1½ cups crumbled feta cheese (preferably Bulgarian or French)

2 tablespoons harissa

⅓ cup lemon juice (from 2 to 3 lemons)

¼ cup extra virgin olive oil

½ teaspoon kosher salt

KOREAN CHOPPED SALAD
WITH SESAME DRESSING

1½ cups short-grain
brown rice

Kosher salt

4 tablespoons canola oil

2 ounces fresh shiitake
mushrooms, stemmed,
caps sliced

2 cups cubed firm tofu
(½-inch cubes)

1 cup Pickled Daikon
Radish (page 145)

1 cup soybean sprouts

⅓ cup toasted salted
sunflower seeds

¼ cup fresh or dried
seaweed (such as hijiki or
toasted nori; see
page 107)

¾ cup Sesame Dressing
(page 52)

1 head romaine lettuce,
outer leaves discarded,
shredded

1 lemon, halved

1 pound black cod fillet,
bones and skin removed,
cut into 4 pieces

4 large eggs

SERVES 4 The fantastic *bi bim bap*, served all over Korea, was the inspiration for this chopped salad, which was designed for the menu at STREET. The dressing was inspired by a house dressing made of toasted sesame oil and Pernod that was served at the three-star restaurant in the South of France where I worked thirty years ago.

1 Put the rice in a medium bowl and rinse it under cold water, stirring it with your hand, for 1 minute. Drain, and put it in a heavy saucepan. Add 2½ cups cold water and ½ teaspoon salt. Cover, and bring the water to a boil over high heat, about 4 minutes. Reduce the heat to low and simmer for 20 minutes, covered, stirring halfway through. Turn off the heat and let the rice steam under the cover for 5 minutes. Then transfer the rice to a large mixing bowl. Fluff it with a fork and set it aside to cool to room temperature. Do not refrigerate!

2 Meanwhile, put 2 tablespoons of the oil in a sauté pan set over high heat. Add the mushrooms and ¼ teaspoon salt and cook, stirring occasionally, until the mushrooms start to brown and are soft throughout, 4 to 5 minutes. Add the mushrooms to the cooled rice. Add the tofu, pickled daikon radish, soybean sprouts, sunflower seeds, seaweed, and sesame dressing. Mix gently to combine.

3 Divide the shredded lettuce among 4 bowls. Squeeze some lemon juice over each bowl, and toss gently. Divide the rice mixture among the 4 bowls.

4 Season the cod with salt. Heat the remaining 2 tablespoons oil in a medium nonstick sauté pan set over medium-high heat. Add the fish and sauté until golden brown, about 4 minutes. Reduce the heat to medium-low. Flip the fish fillets over and cook for 4 to 5 minutes, until the fish is cooked through and starts to flake when lightly

(recipe continues)

pressed. Remove the fish from the pan and put one piece on top of each rice salad.

5 Return the pan to medium-high heat and fry the 4 eggs sunny side up. Season to taste with salt. Top each salad with an egg, and serve immediately. Instruct your guests to break open the egg and mix it into their salads as they are eating.

SESAME DRESSING   MAKES 1¼ CUPS

Juice of 1 medium lemon (about ⅓ cup)

¼ cup low-sodium soy sauce

2 tablespoons rice vinegar

2 tablespoons absinthe

1 (1-inch) piece fresh ginger, peeled and minced

½ cup sesame oil

1 tablespoon spicy sesame oil

In a large bowl, whisk together the lemon juice, soy sauce, vinegar, absinthe, and ginger. While whisking vigorously, slowly drizzle in the oils. Transfer to a container, seal, and store in the refrigerator until ready to use or for up to 3 days. As the dressing sits it will separate, so mix thoroughly before using.

SCANDINAVIAN MIXED GREENS AND APPLES WITH JUNIPER VINAIGRETTE

SERVES 4   The unique, clean flavors of Scandinavia and Eastern Europe have not yet become popular in this country, but I just love them. This juniper vinaigrette is so unusual that when paired with such simple ingredients as apples, Gouda cheese, and greens, it makes this salad unique.

1 Put the lemon juice, olive oil, honey, juniper berries, salt, and pepper in a small bowl and whisk together to combine.

2 Put the watercress, lettuce, frisée, apples, ½ cup of the cheese, the walnuts, and the parsley in a large mixing bowl. Pour the dressing over the top and toss the salad gently.

3 Divide the salad among 4 plates or arrange it on a large platter, and sprinkle the remaining ½ cup cheese over the top.

5 tablespoons lemon juice (from 3 lemons)

¼ cup extra virgin olive oil

1 tablespoon honey

2 teaspoons ground dried juniper berries

½ teaspoon kosher salt

¼ teaspoon freshly ground black pepper

1 bunch fresh watercress, trimmed of thick stems

½ head red-leaf lettuce, torn into small pieces

½ head frisée lettuce or similar chicory green, such as radicchio, torn

2 flavorful firm apples, such as Pink Lady or Arkansas Black, cored and sliced into thin wedges

1 cup shaved or grated aged Gouda cheese

½ cup walnut pieces, toasted

½ cup fresh Italian parsley leaves

JUNIPER BERRIES

These small dried berries take two or three years to ripen from green to a deep blue or purple. Used as a spice, they have a pungent and uniquely piney flavor. Juniper berries can be found in most well-stocked supermarkets.

BABY BEET SALAD
WITH KUMQUAT, MINT, AND CORIANDER

SERVES 4 TO 6 I love growing herbs in my garden. Cilantro is one that is particularly easy to grow, although it tends to flower really quickly. It took me a million years to realize that the seeds on the flowering cilantro plant are coriander. I dried them and they had the most amazing flavor. Next to the cilantro grows my kumquat tree; looking at the fruit one day, I came up with the idea for this dish. The dressing would be delicious on potatoes, cauliflower, or almost any vegetable. If you don't have kumquats, you can substitute fresh limes or oranges or even grapefruit.

1 Trim the beets of their tops and any long roots. Put the beets in medium saucepans (use separate pans for the different colors) and add enough water to cover them entirely. Add 1 tablespoon salt for every 4 cups water, and bring the water to a boil over high heat. Reduce the heat to low and simmer for 30 minutes or until the beets are tender when poked with the tip of a knife. Drain and discard the water. Set the beets aside until they are cool enough to handle.

2 With a kitchen towel or a paper towel, rub the beets to remove the skins (they should slide off easily). Cut each beet into wedges, and put them in a mixing bowl. Add the kumquats and onion.

3 In a separate bowl, combine the mint, coriander seeds, mustard, olive oil, orange juice, lemon juice, and ½ teaspoon salt. Mix well to form a flavorful vinaigrette. Add the vinaigrette to the beet bowl and toss all the ingredients together. Serve at room temperature or chilled.

2 pounds baby beets in assorted colors

Kosher salt

20 kumquats, quartered

1 small red onion, thinly sliced

2 tablespoons chopped fresh mint leaves

1 tablespoon crushed coriander seeds, toasted

1 tablespoon Dijon mustard

¼ cup extra virgin olive oil

½ cup fresh orange juice

Juice of 1 lemon

NOTE Another way to cook beets is this: Preheat your oven to 400°F. Wrap the whole beets, skin on, in aluminum foil. Roast medium beets for 1 to 1½ hours. When they are fork-tender, you can easily rub the skin off with a paper towel. Now they are ready to be used in this or another recipe.

½ small seedless
watermelon (2½ pounds)

½ ripe cantaloupe melon
(1½ pounds)

¼ ripe honeydew melon
(1 pound)

2 (3-inch) pieces young
ginger (see page 209),
peeled and minced
(⅓ cup); or 2 (3-inch)
pieces regular fresh
ginger, peeled and minced
(⅓ cup)

¼ cup sesame seeds,
toasted

¼ cup lime juice (from
3 to 4 limes)

¼ cup low-sodium soy
sauce

½ cup extra virgin
olive oil

2 tablespoons plus
1 teaspoon sugar

1¾ teaspoons kosher salt

1 cup dried green lentils

2 cups wide-flake
unsweetened coconut

1¼ cups blanched raw
peanuts

4 fresh kaffir lime leaves,
chopped (see page 21)

SERVES 6 If it's melon season, you have to make this. In Burma (Myanmar), *gin thoke,* meaning "ginger mix," is a blend of crispy fried garlic, sesame seeds, and ginger, and is eaten as a sweet digestive snack after meals. Although not native to the region, melons are a refreshing and delicious complement to this dressing, together making a perfect summertime side dish. The ginger is key to this salad. Ideally, the gingerroot should be so young that the skin is almost transparent and the roots are tipped with pink.

1 Start by cutting up the melons: Trim off the rind of all 3 melons, remove any seeds, and cut the flesh into ½-inch dice. Put all of the diced melon in a large mixing bowl.

2 In a separate bowl, combine the ginger, sesame seeds, lime juice, soy sauce, ¼ cup of the olive oil, 2 tablespoons of the sugar, and ½ teaspoon of the salt. Mix well and pour over the melon. Toss, and let marinate at room temperature while you prepare the rest of the salad.

3 Put the lentils and 4 cups cold water in a small saucepan set over high heat, and bring to a boil, about 5 minutes. Reduce the heat to low and simmer for 15 minutes. Add 1 teaspoon of the salt and cook for 5 minutes, or until the lentils are tender but not mushy. Drain, rinse with cold water to chill, and then stir into the melon mixture.

4 Combine the coconut, peanuts, kaffir lime, remaining 1 teaspoon sugar, remaining ¼ cup olive oil, and remaining ¼ teaspoon salt in a large sauté pan. Toast the peanut mixture over medium-low heat, stirring it constantly, until the coconut and peanuts have toasted, somewhat unevenly, to a golden brown, 3 to 4 minutes. Remove from the heat and set aside to cool.

5 Just before serving, add the peanut mixture to the melon mixture and stir gently to combine. Serve in a large bowl, preferably at room temperature.

OLIVE BREAD FATTOUSH
WITH JERUSALEM ARTICHOKES

SERVES 4 This is by far the bestselling salad on our STREET menu. When Jerusalem artichokes are unavailable, substitute chickpeas. And if you can't find sumac, substitute additional toasted cumin for it—the dressing is still delicious.

1 Preheat the oven to 350°F.

2 In a small sauté pan, warm the butter, garlic, and ¼ teaspoon of the salt over low heat until the butter becomes frothy. Put the olive bread in a small mixing bowl and pour the butter mixture over it. Toss to coat the bread, and then spread it out in an even layer on an ungreased cookie sheet. Bake for 7 to 10 minutes until the bread is crispy on the outside and slightly soft inside. Set aside to cool.

3 Put a medium skillet over medium-high heat. Add 3 tablespoons of the olive oil, the Jerusalem artichokes, and the remaining ¼ teaspoon salt. Cook, stirring frequently, until the artichokes are browned and tender when poked with the tines of a fork, about 5 minutes.

4 Put the artichokes in a large mixing bowl. Add the olives, cucumbers, tomatoes, parsley, eggs, feta, lemon juice, harissa, the remaining 2 tablespoons olive oil, the sumac, and the cumin and gently toss together.

5 Just before serving, add the bread to the salad, and toss once more.

- 4 tablespoons (½ stick) unsalted butter
- 2 tablespoons chopped garlic
- ½ teaspoon kosher salt
- 4 slices olive bread, torn into bite-size pieces
- 5 tablespoons extra virgin olive oil
- ½ pound Jerusalem artichokes, cut into bite-size pieces
- ⅓ cup pitted Kalamata olives, slivered
- 4 Persian cucumbers, cut into ½-inch-thick half-moons
- 2 medium tomatoes, cored and cut into ½-inch-thick wedges
- 2 cups fresh Italian parsley leaves
- 2 hard-boiled eggs, chopped
- ½ cup crumbled feta cheese
- 5 tablespoons lemon juice (from 3 lemons)
- 1 tablespoon harissa (see page 49)
- 2 teaspoons ground sumac (see page 16)
- 1 teaspoon ground cumin, toasted

JERUSALEM ARTICHOKES

Also called "sunchokes," these small tubers look like knobby potatoes (or sometimes like ginger) but are crunchier, sweeter, and have a slight artichoke flavor.

SAIGON CHICKEN SALAD

CHICKEN

1 stalk lemongrass
(see opposite)

Juice of 3 lemons

¼ cup extra virgin
olive oil

Kosher salt

4 boneless, skinless
chicken breasts

SALAD

4 small tomatoes, cored
and seeded

2 Persian cucumbers,
ends trimmed

1 green papaya (see
opposite), peeled and
cored

1 medium carrot, peeled

½ pound Asian long
beans or regular green
beans, blanched in salted
water

2 cups shredded napa
cabbage

1 cup unsalted peanuts,
toasted

½ cup tightly packed
fresh cilantro leaves

½ cup tightly packed
celery leaves (inner yellow
leaves only)

Nuoc Cham Dressing
(recipe follows)

Butter lettuce leaves, for
serving (optional)

SERVES 4 In the streets and markets of Vietnam, I was introduced to a wonderful fish sauce called *nuoc cham,* which the Vietnamese put on almost everything. I was lucky enough to be invited to the home of a well-known chef, Mrs. Cam Van Dzoan, who showed me how to make it. Her gorgeous house is on the outskirts of Saigon, alongside a river. The lush grounds are full of star fruit, jackfruit, and herbs, and outside the building is an amazing covered professional kitchen. I spent the day learning some of the secrets to Vietnamese cuisine and making a new friend.

1 To prepare the chicken, put the lemongrass on a cutting board. Using the back of a knife, lightly tap up and down the stalk to release the essential oils. Cut off 1 inch of the root end and one-third of the stalk, down from the top, and discard. Cut the remaining stalk in half lengthwise and remove any tough outer layers. Thinly slice and then finely chop the lemongrass. Put it in a medium mixing bowl and add the lemon juice, olive oil, and 1 teaspoon salt. Add the chicken breasts and coat them with the mixture. Cover and let marinate for 20 minutes to 1 hour in the refrigerator.

2 Preheat the oven to 350°F.

3 Remove the chicken breasts from the marinade and put them on a baking sheet. Season with salt and bake for 15 to 20 minutes, until cooked through. (The juices should run clear when the chicken is poked with a fork.) Remove from the oven and let cool slightly. Then shred the chicken by hand into small pieces.

4 To make the salad, cut the tomatoes, cucumbers, papaya, and carrot into thin strips, about ¼ inch thick and 2 inches in length. Put into a large mixing bowl. Cut the beans into 2-inch lengths and add to the bowl. Add the cabbage, peanuts, cilantro, and celery leaves. Add the shredded chicken and dressing and toss all the ingredients together. Serve immediately, either on a platter or individually inside leaves of butter lettuce.

NUOC CHAM DRESSING   MAKES 1 CUP

½ teaspoon Thai shrimp
paste

7 cloves garlic, finely chopped

1 Thai chile, stemmed and
finely chopped

¼ cup lime juice (from 3 limes)

⅓ cup grated coconut palm
sugar (see page 129) or
packed dark brown sugar

¼ cup fish sauce

Wrap the shrimp paste in a small piece of aluminum foil. Using
a pair of tongs, hold the foil package directly over the open
flame of a gas burner (alternatively place it under the broiler
of your oven) for 1 minute to "toast" the paste inside. You will
smell a strong fish odor, but don't worry; it will not translate
to your dressing. Remove the toasted shrimp paste from the
foil and put it in a small mixing bowl. Add the garlic, Thai
chile, lime juice, coconut palm sugar, and fish sauce. Break up
the shrimp paste with the back of a spoon and stir to combine
it with the other ingredients. Serve immediately, or store in an
airtight container in the refrigerator no longer than overnight.

SHRIMP PASTE

Made from fermented, ground shrimp
that are sun-dried and then cut into
fist-size rectangular blocks, shrimp
paste is not intended for immediate
consumption, since it is raw; it
must be fully toasted over an open
flame prior to consumption. It is an
essential ingredient in the foods
of Laos, Thailand, Malaysia, Singapore, Indonesia, and
Vietnam.

LEMONGRASS

A tall grass with a
citrus flavor that's used
in Asian, Filipino, and
other Southeast Asian
cooking, lemongrass can
be used fresh or dried
and powdered. It is
commonly used in teas,
soups, and curries. You
can find it fresh in well-
stocked supermarkets.

GREEN PAPAYA

Green papaya is simply
unripe red or yellow
papaya, and it can be
eaten cooked or raw.
It's often an ingredient
in curries, stews, and
salads throughout Latin
America, Southeast Asia,
and the Caribbean.

INDIAN PUFFED RICE
SALAD

2 to 3 red garnet yams, peeled and cut into ½-inch dice (3 cups)

3 tablespoons extra virgin olive oil

1½ teaspoons kosher salt

1 teaspoon freshly ground black pepper

1 (15.5-ounce) can chickpeas (garbanzo beans), drained

1 small red onion, chopped

1 bunch fresh cilantro, stems and leaves chopped (½ cup)

3 cups *bhel puri* puffed rice

Bhel Puri Dressing (page 65)

SERVES 6 Walking around the streets of India, lined with food stands, you can't help but dive in and eat everything. I did, and boy, it was a cook's dream. There's so much more to Indian food than the samosas and curries we see in the States. Many years ago, on my first trip to Mumbai, I came across an absolutely wonderful street stand serving *bhel puri*, a traditional *chaat* (*chaat* translates as "snack").

1 Preheat the oven to 350°F.

2 In a medium bowl, combine the yams, olive oil, salt, and pepper. Toss to mix, and then spread the yams in a single layer on a baking sheet. Bake for 30 minutes, or until the yams are soft to the touch and slightly browned. Remove from the oven and let cool to room temperature before proceeding.

3 Prepare the salad just before serving, as the puffed rice will become soggy quickly: In a large bowl, combine the cooled yams, chickpeas, red onion, and cilantro. Immediately before serving, add the puffed rice and mix gently to combine the ingredients. Add 1½ cups of the dressing and toss together. Serve with the remaining dressing on the side.

BHEL PURI PUFFED RICE

This type of *chaat,* or Indian savory snack, is usually made by heating rice kernels under high-pressure steam, then spicing them and studding the mixture with crispy crackers and chickpea fritters. At Chowpatty Beach in Mumbai, you'll find a line of stalls all selling *bhel puri*. In the United States you can find *bhel puri* packaged and ready to eat at most Indian markets.

BHEL PURI DRESSING — MAKES 3½ CUPS

2 cups Tamarind Puree
(page 173)

⅓ cup date molasses (see
page 38)

½ teaspoon black salt (see
page 215; optional)

½ teaspoon kosher salt

1 bunch fresh cilantro, stems
and leaves chopped (½ cup)

½ cup packed fresh mint
leaves, chopped

1 (2-inch) piece young
ginger (see page 209),
peeled and chopped

3 tablespoons cumin seeds,
toasted

1   In a medium mixing bowl, stir together the tamarind puree,
date molasses, black salt, kosher salt, and ¾ cup water.

2   In a separate bowl, toss together the cilantro, mint, ginger,
and cumin seeds.

3   In small batches, puree some of the tamarind mix with
some of the herb mix in a blender on high speed. (You
want to do this in small batches to ensure that the herbs
will be pureed finely enough and that all of the ingredients
are well incorporated.) Repeat until all the dressing is
pureed and recombined. Store the dressing in an airtight
container in the refrigerator until ready to use, but not
longer than overnight.

VEGE &

TABLES
GRAINS

THAI CREAMED CORN
WITH COCONUT MILK

1 bunch (about 8) fresh pandan leaves

1 cup heavy cream

1 cup well-shaken canned coconut milk

2 tablespoons canola oil

1 medium white onion, chopped

6 to 8 ears corn, kernels cut off the cob (about 6 cups kernels)

1 teaspoon kosher salt

Puffed Corn Topping (recipe follows)

PANDAN

A dark green straplike grass that has a distinct flavor, somewhat like a briny vanilla, pandan leaves are steeped to infuse the flavor into rice, curries, stews, and desserts in Southeast Asia, Bangladesh, and China. They can be found in Asian markets.

MAKES 6 CUPS Throughout Southeast Asia, the combination of pandan leaves and coconut is used everywhere. Pandan leaves have a very distinct grassy flavor, with undertones of vanilla that complement the sweetness of coconut beautifully. I used this idea and played with a traditional creamed corn to come up with this dish. If fresh corn isn't in season, you can use a high-quality frozen corn. If you want to enhance the dish even further, you could add caramelized pearl onions, peas, and some roasted red peppers.

1 Trim off the white, dirty ends of the pandan leaves and wash the leaves in cold water. Tie the leaves in a knot and place in a small saucepan. Add the cream and coconut milk, set the pan over medium-high heat, and bring the mixture to a boil. Then reduce the heat to low and simmer for 15 to 20 minutes. Turn off the heat and let the mixture cool until the pandan leaves have wilted and the cream mixture has started to thicken.

2 When they are cool enough to handle, take the pandan leaves out of the saucepan, squeeze as much liquid as possible back into the pan, and discard the leaves. The liquid may have a slight green color; that is okay. Set the liquid aside.

3 In a large skillet set over medium-high heat, heat the oil. Add the onion and sauté until it is translucent, 2 to 3 minutes. Add the corn kernels and the salt, and cook for 10 minutes. Then reduce the heat to medium, add the cream mixture, and simmer for 10 to 15 minutes, until the cream has thickened. Remove from the heat.

4 Transfer the mixture to a bowl, top with the puffed corn topping, and serve.

PUFFED CORN TOPPING   MAKES 2 CUPS

3 tablespoons unsalted
butter

¼ cup packed dark brown
sugar

¼ teaspoon kosher salt

Pinch of cayenne pepper

1½ cups puffed yellow corn
or popped popcorn

¾ cup wide-flake
unsweetened coconut

In a sauté pan set over medium-low heat, heat the butter
until it is frothy. Add the brown sugar, salt, and cayenne. Add
the puffed yellow corn and the coconut, and cook until the
coconut is golden brown, about 6 minutes. Remove from the
heat, transfer to a bowl, and let cool.

CACTUS RELLENO
WITH CORN AND ARBOL SALSA

1 pound cactus paddles, cleaned of spines

10 ounces Cotija cheese, grated (about 2 cups)

1 cup cream cheese

1 cup grated Monterey Jack cheese

2 to 3 fresh *hoja santa* leaves (see page 73), finely chopped (optional)

1½ to 2 cups vegetable oil, for frying

2 cups all-purpose flour, for dredging

8 large eggs, beaten

¾ teaspoon kosher salt

Corn Salad (page 72)

Arbol Salsa (page 73)

Sour cream, for garnish

SERVES 8 I learned this dish years ago in Mexico from the mother of one of Border Grill's chefs. She just walked into her backyard and came back with the cactus paddles! After a few lessons on cleaning the spines off the pads, along with a number of needle pricks to my fingers, I became a huge fan of cactus. You should know that cactus is a teeny bit slimy, but this preparation is a great "beginner's course" for the novice nopales eater—a more interesting version of the traditional chiles rellenos, using the cactus pads to hold the cheese.

Prepare the corn salad and arbol salsa up to a day in advance. The cactus cooks quickly, so you'll want to have these two toppings made before starting the cactus recipe.

1 Cut each cactus paddle crosswise into 3 pieces. Then, holding the top of each piece, slice it in half horizontally to open it up like a sandwich.

2 Put the Cotija cheese, cream cheese, Monterey Jack cheese, and *hoja santa* in a small bowl, and mix well to combine. Fill each cactus "sandwich" with 2 tablespoons of the cheese mixture, and then close it by pressing the two sides firmly together. Cover and refrigerate until ready to use. This can be done up to 5 hours in advance.

3 Set a wide sauté pan with 3-inch sides (a cast-iron skillet works well) over medium heat. Fill the pan with enough vegetable oil to reach halfway up the sides. (Remember, the oil will expand and rise as it heats.) Heat the oil for about 5 minutes, or until you hear it starting to crackle slightly and a deep-frying thermometer registers 350°F. Do not let the oil smoke; that will mean the temperature is too high.

4 Put the flour in a shallow dish, and in a separate shallow dish, beat the eggs with the salt. Carefully dip a piece of

(recipe continues)

stuffed cactus into the flour, shaking off any excess but ensuring that the entire surface on both sides is coated. Next, dip the piece into the egg batter until it is completely submerged. Using a pair of tongs, pull the cactus out of the egg and put it in the hot oil. Don't worry if the egg is dripping. Cook for 1 to 2 minutes, until the egg on the bottom side of the cactus begins to brown. Flip it over and cook for 2 minutes to brown the other side. When both sides are browned, the cactus will be cooked and the cheese will be melted. Remove the cactus from the oil and put it on a paper-towel-lined plate to drain. Repeat with the remaining cactus "sandwiches."

5 To serve, pile the cacti on a platter and top with the corn salad, arbol salsa, and sour cream.

CORN SALAD   MAKES 3 CUPS

1 tablespoon canola oil

3 to 4 ears corn, kernels cut off the cob (about 3 cups kernels)

¾ teaspoon kosher salt

½ medium red onion, chopped

½ bunch fresh cilantro, stems and leaves chopped (¼ cup)

3 tablespoons olive oil

Juice of 1 lemon

1 In a skillet over medium-high heat, heat the canola oil. Add the corn and ¼ teaspoon of the salt, and sauté, stirring occasionally, for 3 to 4 minutes, until the corn is cooked and starting to brown. Transfer the corn to a bowl and set it in the refrigerator for 5 to 10 minutes to cool.

2 Add the onion, cilantro, olive oil, lemon juice, and remaining ½ teaspoon salt to the corn. Stir well to combine. Refrigerate until ready to use.

ARBOL SALSA MAKES 2½ CUPS

4 Roma tomatoes

2 tablespoons olive oil

½ medium red onion, thinly sliced

3 cloves garlic

½ cup dried arbol chiles, stemmed and most of the seeds shaken out

1 bunch fresh cilantro, leaves and stems roughly chopped (½ cup)

1½ teaspoons kosher salt

Juice of 2 lemons

1 First, char the tomatoes: Preheat the broiler. Put the tomatoes on a baking sheet and broil, turning them frequently, until the skin is blistered and blackened on all sides, about 3 minutes. Although they will look burnt, the insides will remain juicy and the blackened skin will impart a roasted flavor that adds depth to your salsa.

2 Heat the oil in a small saucepan set over medium heat. Add the onion and cook for 4 to 5 minutes, until the slices are caramelized and dark brown in color. Add the garlic and the arbol chiles, and cook for 2 minutes, being careful not to let the garlic brown. Add the cilantro, tomatoes, and 1½ cups water. Reduce the heat to medium-low and simmer for 10 to 15 minutes, until the vegetables are soft and falling apart. Stir in the salt and lemon juice.

3 Turn off the heat and transfer the mixture to a blender. (You may need to do this in two batches, depending on the size of your blender.) Pulse the blender to let out some steam, and then puree on high speed until the salsa is completely smooth. Pour into a bowl and refrigerate until cool. You may use this salsa either warm or cold.

HOJA SANTA

An aromatic southern Mexican herb with a heart-shaped, velvety leaf and a light anise flavor, *hoja santa* is often used to wrap tamales, cheese, or fish to impart the flavor from its fragrant leaves. If *hoja santa* is not available, substitute anise or fennel seeds.

ROMANIAN
SWEET AND SOUR EGGPLANT

MAKES 4 CUPS; SERVES 4 TO 6 There's a very traditional dish made in home kitchens all throughout Romania and southeastern Europe that's typically called "eggplant salad." I toyed with different ways to highlight the key flavors of the original recipes, which seemed underplayed. I like to make a green salad with watercress, olive oil, and lemon, top it with a scoop of this sweet and sour eggplant, and serve it with a slice of toasted sourdough bread topped with goat cheese and roasted red peppers.

1 Cut off and discard both ends of each eggplant, and cut them lengthwise into ¼-inch-thick slices. Lay the slices out on a baking sheet, and sprinkle both sides with the 3 tablespoons salt. Set aside for 20 minutes so that the salt will draw out some of the water from the eggplant. Then pat the eggplant dry with a dish towel.

2 Put the olive oil, garlic, scallions, parsley, cayenne, and remaining ½ teaspoon salt in a food processor, and puree until a smooth paste forms (it will resemble pesto). Spread liberally all over both sides of the eggplant slices.

3 In a large sauté pan set over medium-high heat, heat 2 tablespoons canola oil. Add enough eggplant slices to cover the bottom of the pan, and cook until they are browned on both sides and cooked through, 2 to 3 minutes per side. Transfer the eggplant to a platter or plate. Repeat this process with the remaining eggplant slices, adding 2 tablespoons oil for each batch. Cut the cooked eggplant into 1-inch-wide strips.

4 In a saucepan set over medium heat, combine the tomatoes, vinegar, and brown sugar. Stew for 12 minutes or until the tomatoes begin breaking down. Add the eggplant strips and stir together. Reduce the heat to low and simmer for 8 to 10 minutes, until most of the liquid has been cooked off. Remove from the heat and serve, or chill. This dish may be served warm or cold.

2 large eggplants (about 2 pounds)

3 tablespoons plus ½ teaspoon kosher salt

½ cup extra virgin olive oil

10 cloves garlic

2 bunches scallions, white and green parts, roughly chopped

½ bunch fresh Italian parsley leaves and small stems, roughly chopped (¼ cup)

½ teaspoon cayenne pepper

Canola oil

1 (14½-ounce) can whole peeled tomatoes, drained and roughly chopped

¾ cup cider vinegar

½ cup packed dark brown sugar

BRUSSELS SPROUTS
WITH GOAT CHEESE, APPLES, AND HAZELNUTS

½ cup hazelnuts

1½ tablespoons extra virgin olive oil

1¼ pounds Brussels sprouts, thinly shaved on a mandoline or with a knife (6 cups)

2 medium Granny Smith apples, cored and diced

1 teaspoon kosher salt

6 ounces soft goat cheese, broken into small pieces

Juice of 1 lemon

SERVES 4 Brussels sprouts are the perfect vegetable to use with a variety of other flavors: their hearty quality pairs well with and stands up to other strong tastes. Here, I've combined them with the sweetness of apple and the richness of goat cheese. Even people who say they hate Brussels sprouts love this dish! The trick with Brussels sprouts is not to overcook them. I like to caramelize them a bit to bring out their natural sweetness but keep the texture firm.

1 Preheat the oven to 350°F.

2 Spread the hazelnuts out on a baking sheet and toast them for 5 to 10 minutes, until they are roasted and slightly browned. Pour onto a clean dish towel. Fold the dish towel over the hazelnuts and roll them around lightly to remove the skins. Discard the skins and then chop the hazelnuts.

3 In a large sauté pan set over medium-high heat, heat the oil. Add the Brussels sprouts, apples, and salt and cook, stirring occasionally, until the Brussels sprouts are slightly browned on the edges, 5 to 7 minutes. Add the hazelnuts, goat cheese, and lemon juice. Toss together and remove from the heat. Serve immediately.

CURRIED SWEET POTATO
PANCAKES

1½ tablespoons cumin seeds

1 teaspoon black mustard seeds

½ teaspoon ground coriander

½ teaspoon ground turmeric

Pinch of cayenne pepper

Pinch of fennel seeds

1 tablespoon minced peeled fresh ginger

¼ cup plus 1 tablespoon canola oil

2 to 3 white onions, chopped (4 cups)

2½ pounds red yams or sweet potatoes, grated (4 cups)

5 tablespoons whole wheat flour

1 large egg, beaten

1½ teaspoons kosher salt

1 cup plain yogurt

½ cup chopped scallions, white and green parts, for garnish

BLACK MUSTARD SEEDS

Small round seeds of the black mustard plant, these are much more pungent than white mustard seeds and used extensively in Indian and other Asian cooking.

MAKES 15 CAKES; SERVES 5 On one of my first trips to India, at a bus stop in Poona, there was a street stand where the vendor was roasting potatoes over charcoal, chopping them, and tossing them with curry spices and crispy onions. He served the mixture wrapped in a piece of newspaper. It was amazing, and it inspired this dish.

There are so many curry spice mixtures from around the world. This recipe employs one of the most common. You can use either yams or sweet potatoes in this recipe.

1 Combine the cumin seeds, mustard seeds, coriander, turmeric, cayenne, fennel seeds, and ginger in a small bowl. Stir well to blend.

2 In a large sauté pan set over medium heat, heat the ¼ cup oil. Add the onions and cook, stirring occasionally, until they are caramelized to a golden brown, 10 to 15 minutes. Reduce the heat to low and add the spice mixture. Cook for 1 to 2 minutes to toast the spices. Transfer the mixture to a bowl. Add the yams, flour, egg, and salt, and mix well to combine. Form the mixture into cakes that are about 3 inches in diameter and ¼ inch thick, and put them on a baking sheet.

3 Set a skillet over medium-low heat and add the remaining 1 tablespoon oil. Working in batches, sauté the cakes for 3 to 4 minutes on each side. They are done when they are a crispy golden brown and the sweet potato is cooked through.

4 Serve warm, topped with the yogurt and scallions.

BLACK KALE CROSTINI
WITH WHITE BEANS AND SPANISH ANCHOVIES

SERVES 12 Years ago, Mary Sue Milliken (my partner at the Border Grill restaurants) and I started working with the Veterans Hospital in Westwood, California, to help develop their horticulture therapy program. We did it partly to help the veterans and partly so that we could get our hands on all sorts of hard-to-find exotic vegetables. The vets grew fantastic produce for us: mizuna, mum greens, sweet potato greens, black mustard seed sprouts, black kale—anything we asked for! They learned how to plant, nurture, pick, sell, and deliver their product, and we were the lucky recipients.

When I traveled to Spain I was finally able to taste the fresh and inventive tapas that the country is so famous for. This combination of a bean paste and anchovies, often with olives, is used in many of the tapas served there. And quite often, the patrons stand while balancing their plates on top of their beer glasses!

1 To prepare the dried beans, put the beans and 10 cups cold water in a small stockpot. Remove any stones or irregular pieces that may float to the top. Bring the water to a boil, and then reduce the heat to low. Simmer for about 1 hour, until the beans are cooked through. Turn off the heat and strain the beans in a colander, reserving the cooking liquid.

2 If you cooked dried beans, wash out the pot and return it to the stove; if you are using canned beans, place a large saucepan on the stove. Set the pan over medium-high heat. Add the oil, and sauté the onion in the oil until it is a deep caramel color, about 5 minutes. Add the jalapeño and cook for 1 to 2 minutes to release the flavor. Add the beans (dried or canned), salt, and 2 cups of the reserved cooking liquid (or 2 cups water if using canned beans).

(recipe continues)

BEANS

2 cups dried white beans, or 1 (14-ounce) can white beans, rinsed and drained

2 tablespoons extra virgin olive oil

1½ cups chopped red onion

1 red jalapeño pepper, stemmed and chopped

½ teaspoon kosher salt

CROUTONS

8 tablespoons (1 stick) unsalted butter, softened

12 white anchovy fillets (sometimes called "boquerones" or "Spanish anchovies"), chopped

½ teaspoon kosher salt

1 small loaf olive bread, sliced into ¼-inch-thick slices

KALE

2 bunches black kale (sometimes called "lacinato" or "Italian" kale)

2 tablespoons extra virgin olive oil

3 cloves garlic, minced

¾ teaspoon kosher salt

Juice of 1 lemon

Stir, then simmer for 10 minutes. Puree until smooth with an immersion blender, or in batches in a regular blender.

3 To make the anchovy croutons, preheat the oven to 350°F.

4 In a small bowl, combine the butter, anchovies, and salt. Mix well with a spoon until all of the ingredients are combined. Spread the mixture on one side of each slice of bread, and arrange in a single layer on a baking sheet.

5 Bake, turning the baking sheet occasionally, for 10 to 15 minutes, until the croutons are crispy and golden brown. Remove from the oven and let cool to room temperature.

6 To prepare the kale, first remove the large stems. Then cut the leaves crosswise into thin strips. Wash them well in cold water to remove any excess dirt. Drain.

7 In a large sauté pan set over medium-low heat, heat the oil. Add the garlic and cook for 2 minutes, until it becomes fragrant but does not color. Raise the heat to medium-high and add the kale and salt. Cook, stirring occasionally so that the kale and garlic do not burn, for 4 to 5 minutes, until the kale is soft but not mushy. Remove the pan from the heat and pour in the lemon juice. Stir well, and pour the kale onto a platter or bowl.

8 To assemble the crostini, take a slice of anchovy toast, spread it with a generous amount of the pureed white beans, and top with the sautéed kale. Set on a platter and repeat with the remaining toasts. Serve while still warm or at room temperature.

INDIAN SAAG
WITH HOMEMADE PANEER

4 tablespoons (½ stick) unsalted butter

2½ cups chopped white onions

1½ tablespoons minced peeled fresh ginger

1 teaspoon minced garlic

1 serrano chile, with seeds, chopped

2 cups chopped tomatoes, with seeds

1¼ tablespoons ground cumin, toasted

1 pound fresh spinach leaves, chopped

2 cups chopped fennel fronds

¾ cup heavy cream

1 teaspoon kosher salt

2 tablespoons extra virgin olive oil

Homemade Paneer (recipe follows), cut into ½-inch cubes

4 cups cooked basmati rice, for serving

SERVES 4 Paneer is a fresh cheese widely used in Indian cooking. Making paneer at home might sound challenging, but it's actually quite easy and takes only about ten minutes. And it's pretty exciting to all of a sudden have homemade cheese in your fridge! All you really need is milk, lemon, and yogurt. You can use paneer in so many great ways: sauté it with spices, use it as a stuffing, or put it in a curry. My friend Alan, who lives in India, showed me this dish. I love how the flavor of the fennel transforms this simple spinach dish from something you get in every Indian restaurant in the United States to a deeply flavorful iteration. This is phenomenal with Curried Lentils (page 116) and Tomato Jam (page 149).

1 Melt the butter in a large heavy-bottomed pot set over medium heat. (A wide pot with low sides will work best.) When the butter is frothy, add the onions. Cook, stirring occasionally, until the onions start to caramelize, 3 to 4 minutes. Add the ginger, garlic, and serrano chile. Cook, stirring, for a minute or so until the mixture is fragrant. Do not let the garlic brown or it will become bitter.

2 Add the tomatoes and cook, stirring occasionally, until all of the liquid has evaporated and the tomatoes are very soft and falling apart, 3 to 4 minutes. Add the cumin. Cook, stirring, for a minute longer, and then add the spinach and fennel fronds. Cook, stirring, for just a few moments to slightly wilt the greens. Reduce the heat to medium-low and add the cream and salt. Cook, stirring occasionally, for 10 minutes, or until the cream reduces and thickens. Turn off the heat.

3 While the greens mixture is cooking, heat the olive oil in a medium sauté pan over medium-high heat. Add the paneer cubes and sauté until they are golden brown on all sides, about 3 minutes.

4 Add the paneer to the greens, and stir well to combine. Serve immediately, accompanied by warm rice.

PANEER MAKES 10 OUNCES CHEESE

2 quarts whole milk

2 teaspoons chaat masala spice blend

2 teaspoons kosher salt

1 cup plain yogurt

Juice of 1 lemon

1 Line a large colander with several layers of damp cheesecloth, letting the edges of the cheesecloth hang over the sides of the colander. Set the colander in the sink.

2 Combine the milk, chaat masala, and salt in a large heavy-bottomed saucepan set over medium heat. Slowly bring the mixture to a boil, 5 to 6 minutes. Just as the milk starts to froth, add the yogurt and the lemon juice. The milk will start to curdle almost immediately. Reduce the heat to low and stir slowly and gently with a wooden spoon to lightly break up the curds and keep them from sinking to the bottom of the pan and burning. Do not break up the curds too much, because larger pieces will produce a softer, better-textured cheese.

3 When the milk mixture appears to be about half curd and has an almost transparent look—after 5 to 8 minutes—pour it into the cheesecloth-lined colander. Pull the edges of the cheesecloth up, wrapping it around the curds. Twist the top of the cheesecloth to expel a good portion of the liquid. When the curds are fairly dry, loosen the cheesecloth and gently press down, using your hands to shape the cheese curds so that they form a flat brick. Remove the cheese curds, still wrapped in cheesecloth, from the colander. Put the wrapped cheese curds on a plate and set another plate on top. Weight down the top plate slightly with a heavy can of soup or other container, to press on the curds, and place this in the refrigerator. Let it chill for at least 1 hour or as long as 24 hours.

4 At this point, you can remove the paneer from the cheesecloth, cut it into cubes, and use them immediately, or you can wrap it in plastic wrap and store it in the refrigerator for up to 5 days.

CHEESE GRITS
WITH THREE PEPPER RELISH

SERVES 4 In the South, grits are often eaten with butter and sugar, but our sous chef at STREET, Jon Beckman, grew up eating grits as a savory side dish with this pepper relish.

1 To make the relish, stir together the honey, soy sauce, Worcestershire sauce, vinegar, and Sriracha in a bowl.

2 Heat the olive oil in a medium sauté pan set over medium-high heat. Add the onion and cook, stirring occasionally, for 5 minutes or until it is starting to color. Reduce the heat to medium-low, add the garlic, and cook for 1 to 2 minutes. Then add the bell pepper, poblano chile, and Fresno chile. Cook for 5 minutes or until all of the peppers are cooked through.

3 Add the honey mixture, reduce the heat to low, and simmer until the liquid has reduced by half, about 15 minutes. Turn off the heat, transfer the relish to a container, and let it cool to room temperature. The relish can be made up to 2 days in advance, refrigerated in an airtight container, and served either hot or cold.

4 To make the grits, in a small saucepan set over high heat, bring 2 cups cold water to a boil. Reduce the heat to low and add the butter and salt. Sprinkle the grits into the water, stirring with a wooden spoon until the mixture thickens and is smooth. Cook for about 10 minutes, stirring frequently to ensure that no lumps form. Add half of the cheese and continue stirring for a few minutes, until the cheese has melted and blended in.

5 Serve the grits immediately, with a spoonful of the pepper relish and a sprinkling of the remaining cheese on each serving.

NOTE Most grits can be cooked, as they are here, with a 4:1 ratio of water to grits. However, always check the cooking instructions on the package, because the grind and cooking time may vary by brand.

RELISH

3 tablespoons honey

2 tablespoons low-sodium soy sauce

1 tablespoon Worcestershire sauce

1 tablespoon cider vinegar

1 teaspoon Green Sriracha Sauce (page 157), or store-bought hot sauce

2 tablespoons extra virgin olive oil

½ medium white onion, chopped (about 1 cup)

2 cloves garlic, minced

1 red bell pepper, stemmed, seeded, and finely chopped

1 poblano chile, stemmed, seeded, and finely chopped

1 Fresno chile or red jalapeño pepper, stemmed and finely chopped

GRITS

2 tablespoons unsalted butter

½ teaspoon kosher salt

½ cup stone-ground grits

½ cup grated Monterey Jack cheese

EGYPTIAN BUS STOP
KUSHARY

3 tablespoons canola oil

2 tablespoons unsalted butter

2 cups chopped white onions

1 cup dried brown lentils, rinsed

¾ cup basmati rice

1 tablespoon ground cumin

Kosher salt

2½ cups vegetable stock or water

1 cup straight-cut macaroni (ditalini)

¼ cup extra virgin olive oil

1 tablespoon harissa (see page 49)

1 bunch fresh Italian parsley leaves, chopped

MAKES 6 CUPS; SERVES 6 TO 8 I learned about this combination of lentils, rice, and pasta in Israel. I was living on a kibbutz outside of Tel Aviv at the end of my junior year in high school, and my friends and I took a week to travel around the country. With no money, we slept on the beaches in sleeping bags and got around by bus. It was at one of the bus stations that I first tasted this dish, which originated in Egypt. I love this method of browning pasta in butter after cooking it, which changes the texture of the pasta, making it firmer and creating a toasted wheat flavor that enhances the dish.

1 In a large saucepan set over medium-high heat, heat the canola oil and butter. Add the onions and cook until they start to caramelize, about 4 minutes. Add the lentils and rice, and toast, stirring constantly, for 5 minutes. Add the cumin and 1 tablespoon salt, and stir to combine. Cook for 1 to 2 minutes to toast the cumin. Then add the stock, reduce the heat to low, and simmer, uncovered, until the liquid has been absorbed and the mixture is starting to crackle and toast on the bottom, about 30 minutes. (You may need to stir the mixture occasionally to make sure that the rice and lentils don't burn on the bottom of the pan. You will know that the mixture is done when the rice and lentils are tender and cooked through, but are not mushy or soft.) Transfer the mixture to a large mixing bowl and set it aside to cool at room temperature.

2 Cook the pasta in a large pot of boiling salted water until al dente. Drain well.

3 Heat a sauté pan over medium heat and add the olive oil. Add the drained pasta and cook until it starts to crisp and brown, 3 to 5 minutes. Remove the pan from the heat, and add the harissa and a pinch of salt (or to taste).

4 Add the pasta and the chopped parsley to the rice mixture, and stir to combine. Serve warm or at room temperature.

WAIPIO VALLEY
SWEET FRIED RICE

MAKES 5 CUPS; SERVES 4 Waipio Valley is a Shangri-la tucked away on the Big Island of Hawaii. There, the taro farms are spectacular. Taro is a starchy root vegetable that's used much like a potato, but it has a more complex, sweet flavor. This vegetable is used all over the world, especially in China in their fried rice dishes. My first memory of tasting authentic fried rice was when—at the tender age of twenty-five, between leaving the Los Angeles produce market at 3 A.M. and waiting for the fish market to open at 6 A.M.—Mary Sue and I went to Paul's Kitchen. It was a dumpy old Chinese diner where all the fish and produce guys went before and after the market—and there I had the most scrumptious fried rice with sweet sausage and a fried egg on top. That was the first time I had ever seen a fried egg on top of rice, and I loved it! But as much as we loved the food, I think the fishmongers and truckers got a bigger kick out of the two of us young female chefs copying everything they ordered!

Chinese rice wine can be found in most Asian supermarkets; it may be labeled "Shaoxing" or "Shao Hsing" cooking wine (from its origins in the region of Shaoxing, in eastern China).

¼ cup low-sodium soy sauce

1½ tablespoons sweet soy sauce

3 tablespoons spicy sesame oil

2 tablespoons Chinese rice wine

1 tablespoon rice wine vinegar

2 tablespoons white sesame seeds, toasted

1½ cups brown rice

1 teaspoon kosher salt

2 tablespoons canola oil

6½ medium carrots, peeled and chopped

¼ pound taro root, peeled and chopped

2½ ounces shiitake mushrooms, stemmed, caps sliced (3 cups)

1 bunch scallions, white and green parts, chopped

¼ cup chopped kimchi (see page 28)

1 (2-inch) piece fresh ginger, peeled and minced

1 Combine the low-sodium soy sauce, sweet soy sauce, sesame oil, rice wine, rice wine vinegar, and sesame seeds in a small bowl.

2 Put the rice in a small saucepan and rinse with cold water for 2 to 3 minutes. Drain, and return to the saucepan. Add 1½ cups water, set the pan over medium-high heat, and bring to a boil, 8 to 10 minutes. Stir the rice gently once or twice, and then reduce the heat to low. Cook for 5 minutes, and then add ½ teaspoon of the salt. Stir once

(recipe continues)

more and cook for 5 minutes. Remove the pan from the heat and fluff the rice with a fork. Transfer it to a mixing bowl.

3 Heat the oil in a skillet or wok over high heat. Add the carrots and taro root, and cook for 2 minutes, stirring constantly to brown the vegetables. Then add the mushrooms and the remaining ½ teaspoon salt. Continue stirring and cooking for a minute or two, until the mushrooms are cooked through. Add the scallions, kimchi, and ginger. Stir and cook for 1 minute more. Add the soy sauce mixture and the rice, and stir thoroughly until all of the ingredients are combined. Reduce the heat to low and cook for 3 minutes to allow the rice to absorb the flavors of the sauce.

4 Divide the fried rice among 4 bowls or arrange it on a large platter, and serve immediately. You can also cool this rice in the refrigerator and reheat it at a later time; it will keep for 2 to 3 days.

COUSCOUS TABBOULEH
WITH DRIED APRICOTS AND PISTACHIOS

SERVES 6 Couscous has a very neutral flavor, but it adds texture and body to any dish. Whenever you make a salad using a grain, remember that the grain will soak up the dressing, so you may need to re-dress the salad on day two. You can use any dried fruit and add even more herbs than I do here.

1 Put the couscous in a medium heatproof glass or metal bowl.

2 Pour 2 cups water into a small saucepan, and add 1 teaspoon of the salt and 2 tablespoons of the olive oil. Bring the water to a boil and immediately turn off the heat. Pour the water over the bowl of couscous, stirring it lightly with a fork, and then tightly cover the bowl with plastic wrap. Let it sit at room temperature for 10 minutes to steam.

3 Remove the plastic wrap and fluff the couscous with a fork until all of the individual grains are separated and there are no large clumps. Put the couscous in the refrigerator and let it cool completely, 20 minutes.

4 After the couscous has cooled, add the remaining ½ cup olive oil and 1 teaspoon salt, the red onion, parsley, mint, apricots, pistachios (if using), and the lemon zest and juice. Mix well with a spoon and serve slightly chilled.

2 cups (13 ounces) couscous

2 teaspoons kosher salt

½ cup plus 2 tablespoons extra virgin olive oil

1 medium red onion, chopped

1 bunch fresh Italian parsley, leaves finely chopped (¾ cup)

1 bunch fresh mint, leaves finely chopped (¾ cup)

1 cup chopped dried apricots

1 cup shelled salted pistachios, toasted and chopped (optional)

Grated zest and juice of 3 lemons

NOTE At holiday time, try using dried cranberries and lots of mint and parsley for a red and green explosion.

LAND

& SEA

TATSUTAGE FRIED CHICKEN WITH SPICY YUZU MAYONNAISE 94

LEBANESE CHICKEN WRAP WITH MARINATED VEGETABLES AND SPICY TAHINI 97

PICADILLO CHILI DOG WITH MUSTARD AND RELISH 99

KOREAN GLAZED SHORT RIBS WITH SESAME AND ASIAN PEAR 100

URUGUAY CHIVITO STEAK AND FRIED EGG SANDWICH 102

CRISPY SHISO SHRIMP IZAKAYA 105

SINGAPORE CRAB CAKES WITH RED CHILE SAUCE 108

MALAYSIAN BLACK PEPPER CLAMS 110

TATSUTAGE FRIED CHICKEN
WITH SPICY YUZU MAYONNAISE

2 cups low-sodium soy sauce

1½ cups mirin (rice wine)

½ cup rice wine vinegar

¼ cup honey, warmed

10 cloves garlic, sliced

1 (3-inch) piece fresh ginger, peeled and chopped

1 (4-pound) whole chicken, cut into 8 pieces

Olive oil spray

¾ cup all-purpose flour, plus more for dredging

⅓ cup rice flour

2 tablespoons furikake (I use noritamago-flavored; see page 96)

½ teaspoon kosher salt

1¼ cups sparkling water

Canola oil, for frying

Spicy Yuzu Mayonnaise (page 154)

SERVES 4   I have to say, I sort of consider myself a connoisseur of crispy chicken because I grew up frying it in an electric cast-iron skillet while standing on a kitchen chair next to my mom. I was the one who got to add in the next piece of chicken when the pieces shrank up enough to make room. My most favorite bites were the pieces of skin that my mom would fry up just for me! *Tatsutage* is Japanese-style fried chicken. The word *tatsuta-age* refers to the frying technique. Here we marinate the chicken in garlic, ginger, soy sauce, mirin, and honey before first baking the chicken. Then with all of those flavors already packed into the meat, the frying procedure becomes all about creating the most perfectly light and crispy coating possible. Made with rice flour and sparkling water, this frying batter has an effervescence that you do not find in typical fried chicken.

1   In a large bowl, combine the soy sauce, mirin, rice wine vinegar, honey, garlic, and ginger. Add the chicken pieces and toss to coat them with the marinade. Cover the bowl, set it in the refrigerator, and let the chicken marinate for 2½ hours.

2   Preheat the oven to 350°F. Spray a baking sheet with olive oil spray.

3   Remove the chicken pieces from the marinade and arrange them, skin side up, on the prepared baking sheet. Bake for 30 minutes, or until the juices run clear when the chicken is poked with the tip of a knife. Transfer the chicken to a plate and set it aside to cool while you prepare the batter.

4   In a medium bowl, whisk together the all-purpose flour, rice flour, furikake, and salt. Slowly whisk in the sparkling water until you have a light, smooth batter.

(recipe continues)

FURIKAKE

A crunchy, dry Japanese condiment that is often sprinkled on top of rice or other ingredients, furikake is usually a blend of sesame seeds, seaweed, red chile, sugar, and salt. It can sometimes contain dried fish, powdered miso, or dried vegetables. The noritamago-flavored variety is made with dried bonito flakes.

5 Fill a 5- to 6-inch-deep heavy-bottomed pot with enough canola oil to reach halfway up the sides. (Remember, the oil will expand and rise as it heats.) Heat the oil over medium heat for 4 to 5 minutes, or until a drop of batter floats immediately and a deep-frying thermometer registers 350°F.

6 Put some all-purpose flour in a shallow bowl. Coat each piece of chicken with the flour, tapping off any excess, and then dip the floured chicken in the batter. Working in batches, drop the battered chicken into the hot oil and fry for 2 to 3 minutes, until golden brown. Remember, the chicken is already cooked—you are simply frying to create a crispy shell. Remove the chicken from the oil and drain it on paper towels.

7 Serve immediately, with the spicy yuzu mayonnaise alongside.

LEBANESE CHICKEN WRAP
WITH MARINATED VEGETABLES AND SPICY TAHINI

SERVES 6 Here's the trick to making a really juicy wrap without having it fall apart: Put a barrier between the wrap and the juicy ingredients, which will prevent the bread from getting soggy. Remember that each ingredient you add to a dish has to be seasoned or else it makes the whole dish flat. So if you are putting watercress as the barrier, as we do in this recipe, dress the watercress to add flavor.

1 In a small bowl, combine the chicken, olive oil, za'atar spice mix, smoked paprika, and 1½ teaspoons salt. Stir well.

2 Pour 2 tablespoons of the canola oil into a medium sauté pan set over medium-high heat. Remove the chicken from the marinade, add it to the pan, and cook, stirring frequently, for 5 minutes, or until cooked through. Transfer the chicken and the oil to a bowl. (Do not discard the oil because it will become a part of the dressing.)

3 Return the pan to the stove, and heat the remaining 1 tablespoon canola oil over medium heat. Add the eggplant and ¼ teaspoon salt. Cook the eggplant, stirring occasionally, until it is soft and lightly browned, 5 minutes. Add it to the bowl holding the cooked chicken.

4 Add the cucumbers, tomatoes, olives, tahini, harissa, and 2 tablespoons of the lemon juice to the chicken and eggplant. Mix well with a spoon to combine.

5 Lay each piece of flatbread over the open flame of a gas burner for about 10 seconds on each side to warm and soften it. Alternatively you can put the flatbread in a 400°F oven for 1 to 2 minutes until warm and soft.

6 In a medium bowl, toss the watercress with the remaining 2 tablespoons lemon juice, and season with salt to taste. Arrange ½ cup of the watercress in a line, horizontally, across each flatbread. Top with ½ cup of the chicken mixture and 3 tablespoons of the yogurt. Roll up the flatbreads, and cut each one in half or in thirds to serve.

¾ pound boneless, skinless chicken breasts, cut into ½-inch cubes

¼ cup extra virgin olive oil

¼ cup Middle Eastern Za'atar Spice Mix (page 169)

1 teaspoon smoked paprika

Kosher salt

3 tablespoons canola oil

½ small eggplant, chopped (about 2 cups)

2 Persian cucumbers, chopped (about 1½ cups)

2 plum tomatoes, cored and chopped

½ cup pitted Greek olives (such as Kalamata), chopped

2 tablespoons tahini

1 tablespoon harissa (see page 49)

4 tablespoons lemon juice

6 pieces lavash flatbread

3 cups fresh watercress or arugula

9 tablespoons plain yogurt

PICADILLO CHILI DOG
WITH MUSTARD AND RELISH

SERVES 8 Picadillo is a chili-like dish that is served in many Latin countries. In Mexico they often use ground beef, onions, tomatoes, and lime, all stuffed into an empanada, while in the Caribbean nations and Atlantic islands they tend to add raisins or fruit. Once I had a version in Puerto Rico with achiote (a citrus-flavored paste made from the seeds of the annatto tree), capers, and olives. This recipe was influenced by my favorite lunch as a kid. My mother made a ground beef, mustard, and raisin mixture that she would scoop onto a hot dog bun and heat under the broiler. I decided to blend it with a new twist for an old all-American dish!

1 Heat the canola oil in a large saucepan set over medium-high heat. Add the onions and cook, stirring occasionally, until they are golden brown, 8 minutes. Add the masa harina, chipotles, cumin seeds, smoked paprika, dry mustard, and cayenne. Stir well and cook for 1 minute to toast the spices. Reduce the heat to medium and add the ground beef and the salt. Cook, stirring and breaking up the beef with the back of a spoon, and scraping the bottom of the pot occasionally so that none of the spices stick and burn, for 8 to 10 minutes, until the meat is browned.

2 Reduce the heat to low. Add the tomatoes and their juices, breaking them up with a spoon so that they're in smaller pieces. Add the currants. Simmer for 35 minutes, stirring occasionally. Add the black beans, stir, and cook for 5 minutes. Remove the pan from the heat.

3 Toast the hot dog buns. Slather the buns with yellow mustard and pickle relish.

4 Heat the olive oil in a sauté pan over medium heat. Add the hot dogs and cook until they are browned on all sides.

5 Put a hot dog in each bun and top with a good amount of the picadillo. Top with more mustard and relish, if desired.

¼ cup canola oil

1½ medium red onions, chopped (2½ cups)

3 tablespoons masa harina

3 canned chipotle chiles, rinsed and chopped

2 tablespoons cumin seeds

2 teaspoons smoked paprika

2 teaspoons dry mustard

¼ teaspoon cayenne pepper

2 pounds ground beef

1½ tablespoons kosher salt

1 (28-ounce) can whole tomatoes, with their juices

¾ cup dried currants or black raisins

1 (15-ounce) can black beans, rinsed and drained

8 hot dog buns

Yellow mustard and pickle relish, for garnish

1 teaspoon olive oil

8 hot dogs or sausages

MASA HARINA

This is the traditional corn flour used to make tortillas, tamales, and other Mexican dishes. I use a fantastic all-natural masa harina from Bob's Red Mill, which you can find at many specialty markets.

KOREAN GLAZED SHORT RIBS
WITH SESAME AND ASIAN PEAR

Olive oil spray

5 pounds flanken-cut beef short ribs, ¾ inch thick

Kosher salt

3 tablespoons canola oil

16 scallions, white and green parts, roughly chopped

10 cloves garlic, sliced

1 (4-inch) piece fresh ginger, peeled and roughly chopped

½ cup sesame seeds

4 Asian pears (see opposite), peeled, cored, and thinly sliced

½ cup mirin (rice wine)

1 cup low-sodium soy sauce

¼ cup spicy sesame oil

1 cup honey

Asian Pear and Celery Salad (recipe follows)

SERVES 4 This glaze has a great balance of sweetness from the Asian pears and richness from the sesame. The trick with cooking short ribs is that they have to contain some fat. I never recommend buying lean meat for braising, as the fat will melt off as it cooks. The fat helps ensure a tender, melt-in-your-mouth result. The cut I think is best for this dish is called flanken—you'll probably have to ask your butcher for it, since it's not commonly set out in meat counters. But it's basically a little longer and thinner than regular-cut short ribs, and cut across the bone as opposed to with the bone. This is the traditional cut used for Korean-style barbecue, and I love the way the marinade and grilling take to it.

1 Preheat the oven to 350°F.

2 Lightly coat 2 rimmed baking sheets with olive oil spray. Lay the ribs out on the baking sheets and season them with kosher salt on both sides. Pour 1 cup water onto the bottom of each baking sheet. Cover the sheets with aluminum foil, carefully put them on the center rack of the oven, and braise the ribs for 1½ hours, rotating the pans about halfway through.

3   While the ribs are braising, make your sauce: Heat the canola oil in a medium saucepan set over medium heat. Add the scallions, garlic, and ginger. Cook for about 5 minutes, stirring frequently, until the scallions soften and the smell of the ginger and garlic is strong. Add the sesame seeds and toast for a minute. Then add the Asian pears. Stir. Reduce the heat to low and add the mirin, soy sauce, and sesame oil. Stir, and let simmer for 25 minutes, stirring occasionally. Add the honey and cook for 5 minutes more. Remove from the heat. Pour the mixture into a blender and puree until smooth (there will be a little bit of texture from the sesame seeds).

4   When the ribs are done, spoon a few heaping tablespoons of the sauce over the top of each one, and spread it out to cover the surface. At this point you can put the ribs on a hot grill to finish or return them to the oven and bake, uncovered, for 10 to 15 minutes, until the glaze browns.

5   Transfer the ribs to a platter and top with the pear and celery salad.

ASIAN PEAR

Crisp, with a grainy texture and high water content, this is sometimes called an "apple pear," though it is not a cross between them. It is best eaten raw, rather than baked into pies or cooked into jams.

ASIAN PEAR AND CELERY SALAD   SERVES 4

3 inner ribs celery with leaves

2 scallions, white and green parts, thinly sliced on the diagonal

2 Asian pears, peeled, cored, and sliced ⅛ inch thick

¼ cup extra virgin olive oil

¼ cup mirin (rice wine)

Juice of 1 lemon

¼ teaspoon kosher salt

Pick off all the celery leaves, keeping the leaves whole. Put the leaves in a medium bowl. Thinly slice the celery ribs on the diagonal, and add them to the bowl. Add the scallions, pears, olive oil, mirin, lemon juice, and salt. Toss gently, and serve immediately.

URUGUAY CHIVITO STEAK
AND FRIED EGG SANDWICH

1½ pounds either flatiron or skirt steak, cut into ¼-inch-thick fajita-style strips

½ bunch fresh cilantro, stems and leaves chopped (¼ cup)

3 tablespoons Worcestershire sauce

2 tablespoons whole-grain mustard

1½ teaspoons kosher salt

3 tablespoons olive oil

2 small red onions, thinly sliced (about 2 cups)

1 red bell pepper, stemmed, seeded, and cut into thin strips

4 large eggs

4 fresh soft-crusted French rolls

8 slices provolone cheese

Golf Salsa (page 104)

4 to 8 slices Spanish-style ham or Italian prosciutto

2 large ripe tomatoes, thinly sliced

SERVES 4   You can see how every country has its own version of common dishes, and they are often very similar to what we have in the United States except for an ingredient or two. This is basically a South American cheesesteak sandwich. Remember the key to a great sandwich: Always make sure that it's sloppy to eat! If it is, it's likely to be fantastic. The Golf Salsa, which at first seems so American, is actually a traditional condiment served throughout Uruguay and Argentina.

1 Combine the steak strips, cilantro, Worcestershire sauce, mustard, and 1 teaspoon of the salt in a large bowl, and let marinate for 15 minutes.

2 Preheat the oven to 400°F.

3 Heat 1 tablespoon of the olive oil in a medium sauté pan set over medium-high heat. Add the onions and cook, stirring occasionally, until they start to caramelize and become golden brown, about 4 minutes. Add the bell pepper and the remaining ½ teaspoon salt. Continue cooking, stirring more frequently, for 3 minutes.

4 Meanwhile, in a separate sauté pan set over high heat, heat 1 tablespoon of the olive oil. Remove the steak from the marinade, add it to the pan, and sear for 3 to 4 minutes, until it is browned. Remove the pan from the heat and add the steak to the onion mixture.

5 Fry the eggs in the remaining 1 tablespoon oil in a nonstick pan until the whites are set but the yolks are still very runny. Transfer to a plate.

6 Cut each roll in half and put them, cut side up, on a baking sheet. Put a slice of cheese on each half of each roll, and put the baking sheet on the center rack of the oven. Bake

(recipe continues)

for 5 minutes, or until the cheese is completely melted and the rolls have started to brown.

7 Remove the rolls from the oven and put one on each plate. Spread some of the salsa over each half of the rolls, and then pile some of the steak mixture over one half. Top with a slice of ham, some tomato slices, and finally a fried egg. Replace the top of the roll, and hold the sandwich together with a bamboo skewer.

GOLF SALSA   MAKES 1 CUP

½ cup ketchup

½ cup mayonnaise

Juice of 1 lime

Combine the ketchup, mayonnaise, and lime juice in a small bowl and whisk together. The salsa will keep in an airtight container in the refrigerator for 4 to 5 days.

CRISPY SHISO SHRIMP
IZAKAYA

SERVES 4 *Izakaya* is the Japanese term for pub food. In the tradition of pubs everywhere, most of the food is served in small portions and complements the wide variety of beer and sake choices. Oddly enough, we got the inspiration for this recipe from a Japanese artist who was working with us in Los Angeles before the opening of the restaurant. Her English was broken, but she told a charming story about her favorite izakaya, which was nori-wrapped shrimp. There aren't too many ways to go wrong with this dish. Just make sure that you set up a production line so the rolling goes quickly. Keep your wrappers covered with a slightly damp towel so they don't dry out. Then, when rolling, wrap the dough tightly so the shrimp stays covered while it's frying.

1 Put the ponzu sauce, daikon, and wasabi paste in a small bowl and stir to combine. Set aside until ready to serve.

2 Run a small paring knife gently along the length of each shrimp, back and front, and then run the shrimp under cold water, using your fingers to devein it. Leave the tail in place. Stretch the shrimp so they lie flat and straight.

3 Put 1 rectangle of lumpia dough lengthwise on the counter in front of you. Lightly brush the entire length of the dough with beaten egg. Sprinkle a scant teaspoon of nori strips along the bottom half of the dough. Sprinkle a teaspoon of the chopped shiso leaves on top of the nori. Place a shrimp horizontally on the bottom half of the dough so that the tail sticks out of the end. Sprinkle the shrimp with salt to taste. Tightly roll the shrimp up in the dough, keeping the shrimp as straight as possible. Just before you reach the end, brush the dough once more with the beaten egg so that the dough seals to itself. Repeat until all the shrimp are wrapped.

(recipe continues)

1 cup ponzu sauce

3 tablespoons grated daikon radish (see page 37)

1 teaspoon prepared wasabi paste

20 large cocktail shrimp, peeled, tails left on

10 sheets lumpia wrapper dough, cut into 2 × 3-inch rectangles

5 large eggs, beaten

2 to 3 sheets nori seaweed (see page 107), cut into thin strips

20 fresh shiso leaves (see page 41), chopped

Kosher salt

About 2 cups canola oil, for frying

LUMPIA WRAPPER

These wrappers, made from flour and water, or from cornstarch, eggs, and water, are sometimes called "Shanghai-style egg roll wrappers." They are thinner than the usual egg roll wrappers and do not fluff up or become airy.

4 Fill a wide 3-inch-deep pan (a cast-iron skillet works best) with enough canola oil to reach halfway up the sides. (Remember, the oil will expand and rise as it heats.) Heat the oil over medium heat for about 5 minutes, or until you hear it starting to crackle slightly and a deep-frying thermometer registers 350°F. Do not let the oil smoke; that will mean the temperature is too high. Fry the shrimp, in batches, until the dough is golden brown and crispy, about 3 to 4 minutes. Transfer the shrimp to paper towels to drain.

5 Put the fried shrimp on a platter and serve with the ponzu sauce for dipping.

NORI

Nori is the Japanese name for edible seaweed sheets that are made by a process of shredding and rack-drying that is similar to papermaking. The seaweed, in fact, looks like sheets of paper and is what encases most sushi rolls. Recently nori has become more popular and it is used in a variety of dishes, from an accent on risotto to the main flavor in ice cream. You can find it in well-stocked supermarkets.

SINGAPORE CRAB CAKES
WITH RED CHILE SAUCE

½ pound Dungeness crabmeat

1 cup ground Japanese rice crackers (3½ ounces) or dry bread crumbs

1 Persian cucumber, chopped (¾ cup)

1 small red onion, finely diced (½ cup)

½ red bell pepper, chopped (¼ cup)

½ cup fresh Thai basil leaves (see opposite), chopped

⅓ cup chopped fresh cilantro

⅓ cup Japanese mayonnaise

2 tablespoons fish sauce

2 tablespoons lime juice (from 2 limes)

¼ teaspoon kosher salt

1 tablespoon canola oil

Singapore Red Chile Sauce (recipe follows)

MAKES 24 MINI CRAB CAKES; SERVES 8 TO 10

Walking through the hawker stands in Singapore City, you are bound to see red chile crabs for sale. Some say it is actually the national dish. Typically you'll see whole crabs, roughly cut in quarters and wok-fried with a red chile sauce. Eating them can be quite a messy experience, so I simplified that dish to turn it into something you might serve for a dinner party or as an appetizer. I love to garnish this with tons of cilantro leaves over the top and a squeeze of fresh lime.

Japanese mayonnaise is different from the stuff we all know in two ways: it is made with egg yolks instead of whole eggs, and with rice wine instead of apple and malt vinegar. It is richer than the usual mayonnaise. Kewpie is the most popular brand available in the United States, and you can find it in Asian or Japanese specialty markets.

1 Put the crabmeat in a medium bowl and check for any bits of shell and cartilage. Add the ground rice crackers, cucumber, onion, bell pepper, Thai basil, cilantro, mayonnaise, fish sauce, lime juice, and salt. Stir together until well combined. Shape into 1-ounce cakes (about 2 tablespoons each).

2 Heat a nonstick skillet over medium-high heat for 2 minutes. Add the canola oil, and arrange the cakes in a single even layer in the pan (do this in batches if necessary). Sear the cakes on both sides, 1 to 2 minutes per side, until browned and warmed through.

3 Transfer the crab cakes to a platter and serve with a side of red chile sauce.

SINGAPORE RED CHILE SAUCE   MAKES 3 CUPS

2 tablespoons canola oil

1 medium red onion, thinly sliced

4 (3-inch) pieces fresh ginger, peeled and roughly chopped (¾ cup)

1¼ cups ketchup

1 cup grated coconut palm sugar (see page 129) or packed dark brown sugar

½ cup chile bean paste (see page 124)

6 tablespoons (¾ stick) unsalted butter

1 Heat the oil in a small saucepan set over medium-high heat for 1 minute. Add the onion and cook for 3 to 4 minutes, until soft and starting to brown. Reduce the heat to medium-low, add the ginger, and continue cooking, stirring occasionally, for 2 to 3 minutes until fragrant. Reduce the heat to low. Add the ketchup, coconut palm sugar, and chile bean paste. Stir, and let simmer for 5 to 10 minutes, stirring occasionally, until the sauce thickens and all of the ingredients have become one cohesive mix. Remove from the heat and transfer to a blender. Pulse to release the steam and then puree on high speed until the mixture is smooth.

2 With a rubber spatula, scrape the sauce back into the saucepan. Set the pan over medium heat and add 1 cup water. Stir well. Let simmer for 3 minutes, and then add the butter, stirring continuously until incorporated. Remove from the heat and serve immediately.

THAI BASIL

Found in Southeast Asia and now—by popular demand—in the United States, Thai basil has small, narrow leaves, purple stems, and mauve flowers. It has an identifiable licorice flavor not present in sweet basil, and its flavor is more stable under high or extended cooking temperatures than that of sweet basil. If you can't find it, you can substitute regular basil.

NOTE If you are making this sauce in advance, stop before adding the butter and refrigerate it, covered, for up to 4 days. Add the butter and reheat just before serving.

MALAYSIAN BLACK PEPPER CLAMS

2½ pounds Manila clams

¼ cup grated coconut palm sugar (see page 129) or packed dark brown sugar

2 teaspoons oyster sauce

2 tablespoons dark soy sauce

Juice of 1½ limes

2 tablespoons canola oil

2 tablespoons chopped garlic

1 (2-inch) piece fresh ginger, peeled and minced

1 tablespoon cracked black pepper

4 tablespoons (½ stick) unsalted butter

10 fresh mint leaves

½ cup fresh cilantro leaves

¼ cup fresh Thai basil leaves (see page 109) or regular basil leaves

Sourdough bread, sliced 1 inch thick and toasted, for serving (optional)

Extra virgin olive oil, for serving (optional)

Lime wedges, for serving

SERVES 4   When I was in Singapore, I got a hot tip from the hotel concierge—after much arm-twisting to *not* send me to a tourist spot—about a great local restaurant. It turned out that her grandfather owned a popular Malaysian diner that was off the beaten path and outside the city. Though there wasn't a lot of English spoken there, as always the love of food was the understood language. That day I tasted lots of traditional Malaysian dishes, including this one, which they made with crab instead of clams. However, the sweetness of clams with this sauce is an undeniably fantastic combination. A big bowl of these clams, the broth, some crusty bread for dipping, and a salad makes the perfect meal with very little mess to clean up afterwards. Whenever we rotate the menu at STREET, we try to take this recipe off and it practically causes a riot.

1 Put the clams in a large bowl and rinse them under cold running water for 5 to 10 minutes to purge them of all sand and grit. Drain.

2 In a small bowl, combine the coconut palm sugar, oyster sauce, soy sauce, and lime juice.

3 Heat the canola oil in a large sauté pan or skillet set over high heat. Add the garlic and ginger and cook for 2 minutes, stirring occasionally, to release the flavors, but do not let the garlic brown. Add the black pepper and the clams. Add ⅓ cup water, cover immediately, and steam the clams for 3 to 4 minutes or until they open. Remove any that do not open. Add the oyster sauce mixture and stir well. Add the butter, stir well, and pour the clams into a large bowl.

4 Sprinkle the mint, cilantro, and Thai basil over the clams. Serve with the toasted bread, brushed with the olive oil, if desired, and wedges of fresh lime.

KOCHI, INDIA

It is better to travel well than to arrive. —BUDDHA

I am traveling lazily down the "back-waters" of Kochi in a slender fifteen-foot wooden boat, with a journalist friend sitting alongside me. Our destination is a small island in the middle of a maze of winding channels, and our intention is to lunch with a coconut farmer. As we pull up to the landing, I see a little pink house surrounded by haphazard vegetable gardens: vanilla bean plants that wind their way up palm trees, gorgeous orchids everywhere, black pepper plants . . . a Shangri-la of my dreams. Thomas, his wife, Leelama, and their twenty-year-old daughter, Jaycee, are the hosts, while a score of neighbors keep dropping by to give or trade some taste or delicacy.

As soon as we arrive, a neighbor offers to take me fishing for mussels, and I immediately accept, eager to get a chance to see mussel fishing in India firsthand. We pole out, and he uses a shovel, which doubles as his pole, to dig down into the mud and bring up the small black shellfish. We return with about fifteen pounds, which will end up being our afternoon snack. They steam the mussels, remove the meat, then salt, fry, and curry them with coconut and spices. They're eaten as a crispy snack, the way we would eat peanuts at a bar. Delicious!

At some point another neighbor comes by, climbs up one of the palms, slices the fronds, and captures the juice in a small jug. This they cork and set aside for it to ferment all day. When it's done, it will be a lovely opaque coconut beer. Another neighbor—you can see how close the community is—brings Thomas a number of freshly caught whole fish in exchange for coconuts. Jaycee, Leelama, and I take the fish to the river to gut and clean them. I spent a year working at a fish market in upstate New York, so it definitely takes me back (although in the United States I worked with a sharper knife!). At this point, what was planned to be a couple of hours for lunch is turning into an entire day spent eating, drinking, and cooking.

Early in the afternoon we take the boat and Thomas shows us the canals. Thomas navigates a low stone bridge—so low we have to lean back in the boat—and then we zigzag our way through ever narrowing canals that are surrounded by acres and acres of palm trees. Thomas stops the boat and we lie back, looking at the canopy of coconut palms above. We doze for an afternoon nap, with nothing to disturb us but the sounds of the river, and eventually return to the house for tea.

Fish curry is to be our next meal, so Thomas shows me how he splits coconuts with one swipe on a hooked spear planted in the ground. This is definitely a honed skill. I help grate the white coconut flesh on a raw steel "fork" attached to the table, while Leelama grinds an amazingly aromatic blend of spices with a stone roller on a stone slab. She throws coconut scraps to their pet parrot while she works. While I'm working away, five ducks waddle around behind me and three curious goats watch the whole process.

Jaycee purees the grated coconut into milk, picks limes from a nearby tree, and takes the paste of ground spices and fries it with garlic and ginger. Meanwhile, Thomas pours us some of his homemade wine. The fish is sautéed in a pan over a wood-burning fire; then the coconut milk and spice paste are added and the whole thing is quickly braised. The dish is finished with rice that was cooked in a hollow bamboo shoot and steamed yucca from their garden.

We put up a folding table among the goats, ducks, orchids, and vanilla beans for a lovely dinner in another world. We've been here so long that the beer has finished fermenting, so we uncork it and drink it along with the meal. The neighbors join us while we talk of politics and overbearing fathers, and after dinner Thomas carves the coconut shells into animal toys for his grandchildren.

At dusk, we pole away from the island, carrying with us twine made from coconut fiber that Thomas sells on the mainland. The river is green and silent except for the water dripping off the poles. Other boats go by occasionally, and people wave or call out a greeting. I could come back here and stay for a month with Thomas and his family, but instead will keep the enchantment of our wonderful food-filled day fresh in my memory.

CURRY & N

& TOFU
OODLES

CURRIED LENTILS
WITH INDIAN DRIED PLUMS

4 tablespoons (½ stick) unsalted butter, or ¼ cup olive oil

2 cups chopped white onions

1½ tablespoons minced garlic

1½ tablespoons minced peeled fresh ginger

3 dried arbol chiles

¼ cup dried kokum plums

6 fresh curry leaves (see page 20)

1 tablespoon black mustard seeds (see page 78)

1 pound (2½ cups) masoor dal (see opposite)

1¼ tablespoons kosher salt

MAKES 7 CUPS; SERVES 10 One of the most eye-opening experiences I had during my first trip to India, twenty-eight years ago, was discovering the huge variety of dals (hulled dried beans, peas, and lentils) and the multitude of preparations using them. Urad dal, masoor dal, lentils—the variety is staggering, and the flavors and colors all differ slightly. The way I learned all of this was by sitting in the kitchen of the ashram in Ahmednagar and cooking with the village women. I came to love their culture and their style; they have a lovely way of respecting each other and greeting each morning. The wildest and most outspoken of these women was named Takubai, and we became fast friends. Even though we couldn't communicate through language, we shared a character trait: sassiness. Takubai is the one who showed me this dish.

KOKUM PLUMS

This dark purple to black sticky fruit with curled edges—which grows in southern India—is usually available as a dried rind that resembles a thick plum skin. When added to food, it imparts a pink to purple color and a sweet-sour taste. Also called "aamsool" or "kokam," it can be found in Indian markets.

1 Heat the butter in a large heavy-bottomed saucepan set over medium-high heat. Add the onions and cook, stirring frequently, until they are caramelized to a rich golden brown, 5 to 6 minutes. Reduce the heat to medium. Add the garlic and cook for a minute. Then add the ginger, arbol chiles, dried plums, curry leaves, and mustard seeds. Cook for 3 minutes, until all the aromas of the spices are released, but do not let the garlic brown.

2 Add the dal and cook, stirring, for 1 minute to toast it with the spices. Then add 7 cups water, stir, and simmer, uncovered, stirring occasionally, for 35 to 45 minutes, until the dal is completely soft and cooked through and has taken on the flavor of the spices.

3 Add the salt and cook for 10 minutes. When finished, the dish will resemble a thick split-pea soup.

4 Serve immediately, or let cool to room temperature, transfer to an airtight container, and store in the refrigerator for up to 4 days.

MASOOR DAL

Found throughout Asia, Southeast Asia, India, and Pakistan, dals are legumes that have been stripped of their outer hulls and split. They cook much more quickly than the whole bean but can be used in any whole bean recipe as a substitute. Masoor dal, also known as "masoor red lentils," is used in this dish, but any lentils can be substituted. It can be found in Middle Eastern and Indian markets, and in well-stocked grocery stores.

COCONUT CURRIED MUSSELS
WITH SMOKY CHORIZO

¼ cup plus 2 tablespoons olive oil

3 cloves garlic

1 small serrano chile, sliced

Grated zest and juice of 1 large orange

½ bunch fresh cilantro

½ bunch fresh parsley

10 fresh curry leaves (see page 20)

1½ teaspoons smoked paprika

2 teaspoons kosher salt

1 medium white onion, thinly sliced (about 1½ cups)

¼ pound dried spicy Spanish-style chorizo, sliced into thin rounds

2 pounds fresh mussels, scrubbed clean and debearded

1½ cups dry white wine

1½ cans coconut milk, well shaken

Juice of 2 limes

Rye or sourdough bread, sliced about 1 inch thick, toasted, and brushed with olive oil, for serving (optional)

SERVES 4 This curry dish is a combination of my favorite flavors. Coming from no one country in particular, it is influenced by the charmoula spice mixes of North Africa, the massaman curry pastes of Thailand, the fresh coconut milk used all over India and Southeast Asia, and my love of smoky Spanish chorizo! It may stray from the authentic in any traditional sense, but it's absolutely fantastic. If you don't have mussels, you can make this dish with whatever you do have—I've even made a vegetarian version with sweet potatoes and fresh mushrooms. If you are improvising with vegetables, sauté them briefly, season them, and then add them to the curry broth.

1 Put the ¼ cup olive oil and the garlic, serrano chile, orange zest and juice, cilantro, parsley, curry leaves, paprika, and 1½ teaspoons salt in a food processor. Puree until the mixture forms a smooth paste. It should make about ½ cup of paste.

2 Heat a very large sauté pan or skillet (the larger and wider the cooking surface, the more evenly the mussels will cook) over medium-high heat. Add the remaining 2 tablespoons olive oil and the onion, and cook for 2 to 3 minutes, until the onion starts to brown. Add the chorizo and cook for 2 minutes, until the sausage is browned and the onion is soft and golden. Add the curry paste and stir constantly for 1 minute.

3 Add the mussels and the wine, and cover the pan immediately. After 1 to 2 minutes, the mussels will start to open. Pour in the coconut milk, stir, and cover again. Cook for 3 minutes to let the flavors meld and the mussels completely open. Uncover the pan, turn off the heat, and add the lime juice and the remaining ½ teaspoon salt.

4 Serve immediately, with the warm toast if desired.

TRINIDAD
DUCK AND POTATO CURRY
WITH PLANTAIN AND GREEN BEANS

SERVES 6 The ingredients in this recipe are almost identical to those used in Indian and Thai kitchens, but the finished dish feels distinctly Caribbean. The method for cooking curries and stews is the same almost everywhere, but the sweet flavors in this curry are amplified by the Caribbean style of cooking with plantains, coconut milk, and mango powder. If you are nervous about working with duck, you can make this curry with chicken—or make a great vegetarian curry using big chunks of sweet potatoes, green beans, whole caramelized shallots, and plantains. I'd love that!

Amchur is powdered sun-dried unripe mango. You can find it in Indian or other Asian markets, or substitute tamarind puree (see page 173)

1 Remove the skin from the duck breasts and legs. Cut each breast crosswise into thirds. Remove the bones from the legs and cut each leg into 2 pieces. You should have 28 pieces total. Season the duck pieces liberally with salt.

2 Preheat the broiler.

3 Put the tomatoes on a baking sheet and broil them, turning them frequently, until the skin is blistered and blackened on all sides, about 5 minutes. Although they will look burnt, the insides will remain juicy and the blackened skin will impart a roasted flavor that adds depth to your curry.

4 Put the tomatoes, skin and all, in a blender and puree until smooth. Add the celery, ginger, turmeric, chile, cilantro, shado beni, curry leaves, garlic, cloves, cumin, amchur, 1 teaspoon salt, and 3 tablespoons water. Pulse the blender a few times to break up any large pieces, and then run it on high speed until the mixture forms a smooth paste.

(recipe continues)

---

4 duck breasts and 8 duck legs

Kosher salt

2 vine-ripened tomatoes

1 rib celery, with leaves, roughly chopped

1 (2-inch) piece fresh ginger, peeled and thinly sliced

1 (½-inch) piece fresh turmeric (see page 122), peeled and roughly sliced, or 1½ teaspoons dried turmeric

½ Scotch bonnet chile

½ bunch fresh cilantro, leaves and stems roughly chopped (⅛ cup)

½ bunch fresh shado beni leaves (¼ cup; see page 171)

¼ cup loosely packed fresh curry leaves (see page 20)

1 clove garlic

4 whole cloves

2½ teaspoons ground cumin

1 teaspoon amchur

4 tablespoons canola oil

2 ripe plantains, cut into small cubes

1 medium red onion, thinly sliced

1½ cans coconut milk, well shaken

Juice of 2 lemons

2 Yukon Gold potatoes (about 1 pound), peeled and cut into thick wedges

¼ pound fresh green beans

Jamaican Ginger Hot Sauce (page 158) or other hot sauce, for serving

FRESH TURMERIC

This yellow-colored root is often used as a key ingredient in curry dishes throughout the Middle East and Southeast Asia and is found in Indian and other Asian markets. It has a hot-pepper-like flavor that is earthy and almost bitter. One of my favorite ways to use fresh turmeric is pureed in a blender with yogurt and honey as a lhassi drink. In general, when you're using it as a spice, you can substitute dry turmeric, but for the lhassi, you need it to be fresh.

5 Heat 3 tablespoons of the oil in a small stockpot set over medium-high heat. Working in batches, sear the duck pieces for 2 to 3 minutes on each side, until golden brown. Transfer the duck to a plate, leaving any fat and juices in the pot.

6 Add the plantains to the same pot and cook until golden brown on all sides, about 4 minutes. Transfer to a plate.

7 Again in the same pot, add the remaining 1 tablespoon oil and the onion. Cook, stirring frequently, until the onion starts to brown, 3 minutes. Add the curry paste. Continue to cook, stirring constantly, for 4 to 5 minutes to toast the curry paste slightly.

8 Reduce the heat to medium-low. Add 3 cups water and the coconut milk, lemon juice, 1½ teaspoons salt, and the potatoes. Stir. Add the seared duck and simmer the curry, uncovered, for 30 minutes. The curry should not be bubbling rapidly. Reduce the heat if needed and stir occasionally so that the ingredients don't settle to the bottom of the pot.

9 Add the green beans and the seared plantains and cook for 10 minutes, or until both the duck meat and the potatoes are tender.

10 Divide the curry among 6 bowls and top each with a spoonful of the hot sauce.

SZECHUAN TOFU
WITH MABO PORK AND ASIAN GREENS

SERVES 6 This Chinese street food dish will turn you into a tofu lover if you're not one already. It can be found in dim sum restaurants all across the country and is a simple, warm, comfort-food kind of meal with just the right amount of spice. It is a great alternative to a soup or noodle dish on a cold day. I make this dish with ground chicken too, and honestly it tastes almost the same—so for those of you who don't eat pork, try it with chicken. I love to serve this with a side of Pickled Daikon Radish (page 145).

1 Put the pork and the five-spice marinade in a medium bowl. Mix well with your hands so that the meat is evenly coated, but do not overmix or the meat will get chewy.

2 In a large sauté pan set over medium-high heat, heat 2 tablespoons of the oil. Add the marinated pork, reduce the heat to medium, and cook, stirring occasionally and breaking up the pork with the back of a spoon, for about 5 minutes, or until the pork is browned through. Transfer the pork to a paper-towel-lined plate to drain.

3 Wash the sauté pan and return it to the stove. With the heat on medium-high, add the remaining 2 tablespoons canola oil and heat it for about a minute, until hot. Then put the tofu in the pan and cook for 3 to 4 minutes, until browned on all sides. Add the yu choy greens and cook for 2 minutes. Add the cooked pork and the mabo sauce and cook for 2 minutes. Turn off the heat, and serve immediately over warm rice.

DARK SOY SAUCE

Slightly thicker, aged longer, and containing added molasses, dark soy sauce has a richer, sweeter, less salty flavor than the usual light soy sauce. It can be found in Chinese specialty markets.

1½ **pounds ground pork**

½ **cup Five-Spice Marinade (page 161)**

4 **tablespoons canola oil**

13 **ounces firm dry-packed tofu cutlets (or two 10-ounce packages firm wet-packed tofu), cut into ½-inch cubes**

1½ **pounds yu choy greens or any Asian stir-fry greens, chopped**

3 **cups Mabo Tofu Sauce (page 124)**

6 **cups cooked rice, warm**

YU CHOY GREENS

This leafy green vegetable, often referred to as "green choy sum," is related to bok choy. Grown mainly for the young leaves and the flowering stalks, it is used for stir-frying in Southeast Asia and China. Substitute any sturdy, dark leafy greens or regular bok choy if you cannot find it.

FERMENTED SOYBEANS

Traditionally used in making Chinese black bean sauce, fermented soybeans have a flavor that is at once sharp, salty, and bitter. The fermentation and salting process is what turns the soybeans black and soft. In Chinese cuisine, fermented soybeans are often used for flavoring fish and stir-fried vegetables. Also called "Chinese fermented black beans" or "douchi."

MABO TOFU SAUCE   MAKES 3 CUPS

1 cup Chinese rice wine (see page 89)

⅔ cup chile bean paste

⅓ cup hoisin sauce

2 tablespoons rice wine vinegar

2 tablespoons fermented soybeans, rinsed

2 tablespoons low-sodium soy sauce

1 tablespoon dark soy sauce (see page 123)

1 teaspoon red chile flakes

1 (2-inch) piece fresh ginger, peeled and minced

In a medium mixing bowl, combine the rice wine, chile bean paste, hoisin sauce, rice wine vinegar, fermented soybeans, low-sodium and dark soy sauces, red chile flakes, and ginger. Mix with a spoon and then cover tightly with plastic wrap. Let sit for at least 1 hour at room temperature or overnight in the refrigerator for the flavors to meld.

CHILE BEAN PASTE

This spicy, salty paste made from a fermented mixture of broad beans, soybeans, salt, rice, and red chile peppers, is also known as "toban djan" or "doubanjiang." It is commonly referred to as "the soul of Szechuan cuisine." It can be found in most Asian markets that specialize in Chinese ingredients.

CHILLED SOBA NOODLES
WITH SPICY ORANGE SESAME AND TOFU

4 cups fresh orange juice

1 (12.7-ounce) package soba noodles

⅓ cup low-sodium soy sauce

⅓ cup spicy sesame oil

⅓ cup sugar

¼ cup rice wine vinegar

2 tablespoons black sesame seeds, toasted

1 bunch scallions, white and green parts, thinly sliced on the diagonal

1 (10-ounce) package firm tofu, cut into small cubes and salted to taste

SERVES 4 I'm always blown away by how few people in the United States think about cooking with buckwheat noodles. Soba noodles have a wonderful earthy, almost sweet taste and are sturdier than noodles made from wheat. This tangy orange and sesame dressing is the perfect partner for this fantastic noodle.

1 Pour the orange juice into a small saucepan set over medium-high heat, and bring to a boil. Then reduce the heat to low and simmer for 30 to 40 minutes, or until the orange juice is thick and syrupy and has reduced to 1 cup.

2 While the orange juice is simmering, cook your noodles: Bring a large pot of water to a boil. (The general ratio for cooking noodles is 4 quarts of water per pound of noodles.) Add the noodles to the boiling water and stir well. Reduce the heat to medium-low and cook for 5 minutes, stirring occasionally. Drain the noodles and rinse them twice with cold water. Drain well, and transfer them to a bowl.

3 When your orange juice is ready, remove the pan from the heat. Pour the syrupy juice into a blender, and add the soy sauce, sesame oil, sugar, and rice wine vinegar. Puree until smooth and emulsified, about 2 minutes. Pour half of the dressing over the noodles and toss well to combine. Put the noodles in the refrigerator to cool, 20 to 30 minutes.

4 Toss the cooled noodles with the toasted black sesame seeds and sliced scallions. Top with the tofu, and serve with the remaining dressing on the side.

INDONESIAN TEK-TEK NOODLES
WITH CHOPPED PEANUT SAUCE

SERVES 4 "Tek-tek" refers to the sound you hear when a woodpecker pecks on a tree. Indonesian street vendors serving tek-tek will often hit their wooden spoons on their carts so people know they've arrived. I use peanut, tamarind, and ginger in my tek-tek, though typically, Indonesians might use ground candlenut (a thickening agent) and kencur (a bitter root in the ginger family).

1 Bring a large pot of water to a boil, and season it with 1 tablespoon of the salt. (The general rule of thumb for cooking noodles is to use 4 quarts of water for every pound of noodles.) Add the noodles and cook, stirring occasionally, for 2 minutes. Drain in a colander and set aside until ready to use.

2 Heat 2 tablespoons of the oil in a large skillet set over medium-high heat. Add the eggplants and ½ teaspoon of the salt, and cook for 1 to 2 minutes, until slightly golden. Then add the carrot, long beans, bell pepper, and ½ teaspoon of the salt, and cook, stirring occasionally, for 2 minutes or until the vegetables are browned. Add the bok choy and the remaining ½ teaspoon salt and cook for 3 to 4 minutes. All the vegetables should be cooked through but not overly soft. Transfer the vegetables to a bowl, and add the tofu.

3 Return the same skillet to the stove over medium-high heat, and make sure it gets hot before proceeding. Add 2 tablespoons oil and then, working very quickly and stirring continuously, add the noodles, the orange juice, then half of the tek-tek sauce, and then the vegetable-tofu mixture. This entire process will take only 2 to 3 minutes. Turn off the heat and stir in the remaining tek-tek sauce.

(recipe continues)

1½ tablespoons kosher salt

1 (1-pound) package mi chay noodles (wide yakisoba-style wheat noodles)

6 tablespoons canola oil

2 small Japanese eggplants or 1 small regular eggplant, cut into thin strips

1 medium carrot, peeled and cut into thin strips

10 Asian long beans, or ¼ pound green beans, cut into 3-inch pieces

½ red bell pepper, cut into thin strips

6 heads baby bok choy, quartered lengthwise

¼ pound firm dry-packed tofu cutlets, cut into thin strips

Juice of 1 orange

1 cup Tek-Tek Sauce (page 129)

4 large eggs

4 Heat a nonstick skillet over low heat. Pour the remaining 2 tablespoons oil into the skillet and swirl to coat the pan. Crack the eggs into the pan and let them sit and slowly cook for 4 to 5 minutes. The oil should not crackle and the eggs should cook slowly. It will take a little longer, but the end result will be eggs that have a tender white and a perfectly soft yellow yolk.

5 Divide the noodles among 4 bowls and top each one with a fried egg. Serve immediately.

TEK-TEK SAUCE MAKES ¾ CUP

¼ cup all-natural peanut butter, at room temperature

2 tablespoons rice wine vinegar

2 tablespoons Tamarind Puree (page 173)

2 tablespoons low-sodium soy sauce

1 tablespoon sweet soy sauce (optional)

2 tablespoons grated coconut palm sugar or packed dark brown sugar

1½ tablespoons tahini

4 dried arbol chiles, broken into pieces and seeds removed

1 (2-inch) piece fresh ginger, peeled and thinly sliced

½ teaspoon ground turmeric

Pour ¼ cup warm water into a blender. Add the peanut butter, vinegar, tamarind puree, low-sodium soy sauce, sweet soy sauce (if using), coconut palm sugar, tahini, chiles, ginger, and turmeric, and puree until completely smooth. Using a rubber spatula, scrape the sauce into a small bowl, and set it aside until ready to use. The sauce can be made up to 1 day in advance and stored in an airtight container in the refrigerator.

PALM SUGAR OR COCONUT PALM SUGAR

Used in Southeast Asia, India, and South America, all palm sugars these days are made from the sap of the coconut palm tree—although the labels will differ, with or without the word "coconut." Coconut palm sugar is golden brown and is sold as granules, blocks, or a liquid. It may be light colored or dark, soft and gooey or hard. If you can't find granules, the bricks are easy to grate on a box grater. If necessary, substitute dark brown sugar.

THAI DRUNKEN SHRIMP
WITH RICE NOODLES

1½ pounds wide-cut flat rice noodles

½ pound large cocktail shrimp, peeled and deveined, tails removed, cut in half crosswise

¼ cup Chinese rice wine (see page 89)

2 tablespoons Five-Spice Marinade (page 161)

2 tablespoons grated coconut palm sugar (see page 129) or packed dark brown sugar

2 tablespoons fish sauce

Juice of 3 limes

¾ teaspoon kosher salt

6 stalks yu choy greens (see page 123) or bok choy

¼ head napa cabbage, thinly sliced (2 cups)

2 inner ribs celery with leaves, thinly sliced

2 plum tomatoes, each cut into 6 wedges

1 cup loosely packed fresh cilantro leaves

15 fresh mint leaves

½ cup fresh Thai basil leaves (see page 109) or regular basil leaves

3 tablespoons canola oil

2 red jalapeño peppers or Fresno chiles, sliced

1 (2-inch) piece fresh ginger, peeled and minced

3 cloves garlic, minced

2 tablespoons (about 2 strands) Thai green peppercorns in brine (see page 132)

SERVES 4 TO 6 This dish gets its name from the rice wine used to marinate the shrimp. The combination of fish sauce, lime, coconut palm sugar, and basil is typical in Thai cooking. These ingredients also make a dressing that can be used on fruit and nut combinations, or on a salad of cucumbers and Chinese sausage, or on green papaya, giving them all a wonderful Thai flavor profile.

1 Soak the rice noodles in a large bowl of very warm water for 30 minutes.

2 At the same time, put the shrimp, rice wine, five-spice marinade, coconut palm sugar, fish sauce, lime juice, and ½ teaspoon of the salt in a bowl. Stir, and then put in the refrigerator to marinate for 30 minutes.

3 Meanwhile, prepare the vegetables: Remove the thick ends from the yu choy greens and cut the greens into 1-inch-wide diagonal slices. Wash the greens, drain them, and put them in a large mixing bowl. Add the cabbage, celery, tomato wedges, cilantro, mint, and Thai basil.

4 Once the noodles have soaked, delicately lift each folded noodle section from the water. Because of the way they come packaged, it is important to separate them carefully so that they do not break. Keep them in the water until all the noodles are soft, and then drain in a colander. Set aside until ready to use.

5 Heat a very large sauté pan or skillet (the larger and wider the cooking surface, the more evenly the noodles will cook) over high heat. Add 2 tablespoons of the oil and reduce the heat to medium-high. Add the peppers, ginger, garlic, and green peppercorns, and cook for 1 minute to toast. Add the bowl of vegetables and herbs, and the remaining ¼ teaspoon salt. While stirring constantly, cook quickly for 1 to 2 minutes, until the vegetables are lightly cooked. Transfer the vegetables to a bowl.

(recipe continues)

THAI GREEN PEPPERCORNS

Thai cuisine often uses fresh green peppercorns, which are usually stored in brine. They taste like a mix of peppercorns and capers, and are typically used in stir-fried dishes and in certain curries and noodle dishes. Peppercorns are used to acidify and balance a rich dish. You can substitute dried pink peppercorns if need be.

6   Return the sauté pan to the stove over high heat. Add the remaining 1 tablespoon oil and the shrimp, reserving the marinade, and sauté quickly for 1 minute. Then add the cooked vegetables and lay the noodles on top of them. Add the reserved shrimp marinade. Do not stir for 2 minutes; the noodles will soften from the steam. Then, using a rubber spatula or a wok spatula, gently fold the noodles and other ingredients together a few times to coat everything with the sauce. Continue to cook for 2 to 3 minutes, or just enough time for the noodles to cook through.

7   Remove from the heat and pour onto a platter. Serve immediately.

STUFFED BITTER MELON SOUP
WITH VERMICELLI RICE NOODLES

SERVES 4 I first saw bitter melon in the markets of India but have since seen it in Vietnam as well. You never forget this vegetable because it is so odd looking! And you never forget the first taste of it because it is very, very bitter. The first time I tasted this soup in Ho Chi Minh City, my guide, Captain Cook, laughed so hard at my expression that he almost wet his pants. But since then I've grown to love it. The bitterness of the melon permeates this entire soup, so if you are unfamiliar with this flavor, you may want to try the version that substitutes zucchini. But if you are someone who leans toward bitter, you have to try this.

1 Put the noodle broth, rock sugar, and star anise in a large saucepan and cook over medium heat, stirring occasionally, until the rock sugar dissolves, 5 to 10 minutes. Turn off the heat and stir in 1 tablespoon of the fish sauce and 1 teaspoon salt. Strain, then keep warm until needed.

2 In a small mixing bowl, combine the ground pork, half of the scallions, the ginger, coriander, garlic, remaining tablespoon of fish sauce, and the egg white. Mix well with your hands to incorporate all of the ingredients evenly.

3 Wash the bitter melon, cut off each end, and cut into thirds, so that you have 3 short, round "towers." Using a small knife, scoop out the pale white center and seeds of each piece. (If using zucchini, do the same, but skip the next step; you do not need to blanch the zucchini.)

4 Bring a large pot of water to a boil (the more water, the more the bitterness will be removed) and set a bowl of ice water beside it. Add 2 tablespoons salt for every 4 quarts of water. Blanch the bitter melon by dropping it in the boiling water and leaving it for 3 minutes. Remove the melon from the pot and drop it into the bowl of ice water. Once it has cooled, remove it from the ice water and pat dry.

(recipe continues)

Ingredients

4 cups Basic Noodle Broth (page 136) or store-bought low-sodium chicken broth

1 (1-inch) chunk rock sugar (see page 136)

2 whole star anise

2 tablespoons fish sauce

Kosher salt

5 ounces ground pork

4 scallions, white and green parts, finely chopped

1 (2-inch) piece fresh ginger, peeled and minced

¼ teaspoon ground coriander

1 clove garlic, minced

1 large egg white

1 pound bitter melon (about 3 medium; see page 135), or 3 medium zucchini

6 ounces dried Vietnamese vermicelli-style noodles (bun tu'oi dac biet)

2 cups mung bean sprouts (optional)

8 limes, cut into wedges

1 bunch fresh shado beni leaves (see page 171)

1 bunch fresh cilantro, tender stems and leaves

Leaves from 1 bunch fresh Thai basil (see page 109) or regular basil

Leaves from 1 bunch fresh mint

5 Fill each "tower" of bitter melon with about 3 tablespoons of the pork filling, keeping a ¼-inch space at each end to allow room for the filling to expand while cooking.

6 Bring a large pot of water to a boil (at least 4 quarts). Add the noodles and cook, stirring continually, for 5 minutes. Turn off the heat and let them sit for 1 minute longer in the water. Then drain and rinse with cold water.

7 In a large saucepan, bring the broth to a boil over high heat. Reduce the heat to medium-low and add the stuffed bitter melons, laying them on their sides. Let simmer for 20 minutes, turning the melons every so often to cook on all sides. When the pork filling is cooked all the way through, it may still have a slightly pink tone from being poached instead of roasted. Remove the melons and cut them into ½-inch-thick slices. Reserve the hot broth.

8 To serve, put ½ cup of the cooked noodles in the center of each of 4 large soup bowls. Lay 4 to 5 slices of the stuffed bitter melon around the noodles. Ladle 1 cup of the hot soup broth over the top. Serve with a platter of the mung bean sprouts, lime wedges, shado beni, cilantro, basil, mint, and the remaining 2 scallions. Instruct your guests to squeeze the lime over the top and add the other ingredients before eating.

BITTER MELON

A very bitter fruit with a warty exterior, this is usually eaten green (not fully ripe); it turns yellow when fully ripe. It is hollow in cross-section, with a thin layer of flesh surrounding a central seed cavity filled with large flat seeds and pith, which are removed before cooking. Bitter melon is used extensively in Southeast Asian, Indian, Pakistani, and Bangladeshi cooking.

ROCK SUGAR

Also known as "yellow rock sugar" or "rock candy," this is crystallized cane sugar, pale brown in color and with a slight caramel flavor. It can be found in most Asian markets and is a traditional ingredient in Vietnamese soup broths.

DASHI KOMBU

A type of kelp or seaweed, kombu is one of the three main ingredients needed to make dashi, a soup stock common in Japan. It imparts a grassy, earthy flavor that has subtle ocean undertones. It adds a depth of flavor that is hard to articulate, but transforms simple broths into something spectacular. You can find dashi kombu (dried kombu) in Asian specialty markets and through online suppliers.

BASIC NOODLE BROTH (2¾ QUARTS)
MAKES 11 CUPS

3 pounds chicken legs

2½ pounds pork bones

2 Chinese leeks, white and light green parts, cut into 2- to 3-inch pieces (or substitute 3 regular leeks and 2 cloves garlic)

2¼ cups (2 ounces) dried shiitake mushrooms

2 (4 × 6-inch) strips (1½ ounces) dashi kombu

1 (3-inch) piece fresh ginger, peeled and sliced

1½ tablespoons kosher salt

This wonderful clear broth is the foundation of all of our soups and noodle broths at the restaurant (except for the vegetarian ones). It has a much more complex flavor than an ordinary chicken or beef stock. Starting with this broth, you can make many dishes by adding any type of noodles or rice, or a myriad of vegetables. You can even poach any protein in it for a heartier soup. Once it's chilled, put it into small containers and freeze them so you can pull them out to use whenever you want to quickly throw a soup together. If you don't have time to make this broth from scratch, you can buy chicken stock in a can or carton and amp up its flavor by adding kombu (seaweed), dried shiitake mushrooms, and fresh ginger.

1 Put the chicken legs, pork bones, leeks, dried mushrooms, dashi kombu, ginger, and salt into a medium stockpot, add water just to cover, and set over high heat. Bring to a boil and then reduce the heat to low. Simmer slowly for 1 hour. As the stock is simmering, skim off and discard any foam and impurities that float to the top. Keep your ladle and bowl close by because you'll continue to skim several times throughout the cooking process.

2 Turn off the heat and strain the stock through a fine-mesh strainer into a bowl, discarding the solids. Let cool; then cover and refrigerate or freeze.

DITALINI PASTA WITH ROMAN BROCCOLI, WHITE BEANS, AND PECORINO

SERVES 4 On my first trip to Italy, I fell in love with the delicious broccoli rabe, also known as rapini, cooked slowly in extra virgin olive oil and served over pasta. I like ditalini, which is a small tube-shaped pasta, for this dish because it's small enough to fit in your spoon with both the broccoli and the white beans. That means that every bite will have all the flavors. Sometimes I'll eat this in the morning, reheated and topped with a fried egg!

1 cup dried white beans

2 ribs celery, cut into thirds

1 small carrot, peeled and cut into thirds

2 cloves garlic

Kosher salt

1 pound broccoli rabe

¼ cup plus 2 tablespoons extra virgin olive oil, plus extra for tossing

2 tablespoons chopped garlic (6 cloves)

¼ teaspoon cayenne pepper

2 cups ditalini pasta, or any small pasta

1 cup grated pecorino cheese

Juice of ½ lemon

1 In a large saucepan set over high heat, combine the beans, celery, carrot, and whole garlic cloves. Cover with 10 cups water, and bring to a boil over high heat. Reduce the heat to medium-low and simmer for 30 minutes. Add 1 tablespoon salt and cook for another 30 minutes or until the beans are tender. Drain off the liquid and discard the pieces of carrot, celery, and garlic.

2 While the beans are cooking, prepare the broccoli rabe: Cut off and discard the bottom 2 inches (the thick ends) of the broccoli rabe. Cut the rest of the broccoli rabe into 2-inch pieces. Put it into a heavy-bottomed pot set over very low heat, and add the ¼ cup olive oil, the chopped garlic, the cayenne, and 1 teaspoon salt. Stir well, cover, and let cook for 15 minutes. The trick to keeping the broccoli rabe from becoming too bitter is to take your time and cook it slowly and evenly.

3 Add the 2 tablespoons olive oil and 3 tablespoons of water to the broccoli rabe. Stir, cover again, and cook for 8 minutes. It will appear overcooked and almost mushy—this is exactly what you're looking for. Turn off the heat, leave the pan covered, and let the mixture steam for 10 minutes.

(recipe continues)

4 Meanwhile, in a large pot, bring 6 cups water and 1 tablespoon salt to a boil. Add the pasta and cook for 12 minutes or until al dente. Drain, toss lightly in olive oil to coat, and then spread the pasta out on a baking sheet to cool.

5 When you're ready to serve the dish, combine the pasta, broccoli rabe, and beans in a large bowl. Add ½ cup of the pecorino cheese and the lemon juice. Stir well to combine. Put the pasta mixture in a large serving bowl, or divide it among 4 smaller bowls. Garnish with the remaining ½ cup pecorino.

ANATOLIAN RAVIOLI
WITH CHICKPEAS, FETA, AND BROWN BUTTER

⅓ pound kataifi pastry dough (see opposite; optional)

3 tablespoons unsalted butter, melted

Kosher salt

2 tablespoons extra virgin olive oil

1 large white onion, finely chopped

1 pound cremini or button mushrooms, finely chopped (5 cups)

1 teaspoon smoked paprika

1 (12-ounce) package square wonton wrappers

3 large eggs, beaten

Smoked Paprika Butter (recipe follows)

1 (15.5-ounce) can chickpeas (garbanzo beans), rinsed and drained

2 lemons, halved

Mint Yogurt (recipe follows)

¼ cup crumbled feta cheese

MAKES 30 RAVIOLI; SERVES 6 I spent a summer on the Greek island of Patmos, in a tiny house in the middle of an olive grove. This pasta dish, finished with brown butter and feta, was first made for me by the olive farmer who lived next door. When the ravioli is lightly coated in this toasty, smoky, spicy butter, then finished with minted yogurt, you will honestly think you've gone to heaven . . . or to the Mediterranean.

1 If you are making the dish with the kataifi pastry, preheat the oven to 400°F.

2 Put the kataifi dough in a small mixing bowl, and using your hands, pull apart the ribbons to separate them slightly. Add the melted butter and a pinch of salt. Mix well, and then spread it out on a baking sheet. Bake, stirring about halfway through, for 10 to 12 minutes, until golden brown. Set aside to cool.

3 Meanwhile, make the ravioli filling: Heat the olive oil in a medium sauté pan set over medium-high heat. Add the onion and cook, stirring occasionally, until it starts to brown, about 4 minutes. Add the mushrooms, smoked paprika, and 2 teaspoons salt. Cook for 3 to 4 minutes, stirring frequently. Remove from the heat, transfer to a bowl, and place in the refrigerator to cool.

4 To assemble the ravioli, spread 30 wonton wrappers out on a work surface, and brush them with the beaten eggs, covering them completely. Put 1 level tablespoon of the mushroom mixture in the center of each wrapper. Fold up each wrapper so all four corners meet in the center. Then pinch the edges of the dough together so that, when you look down on it, the pinched edges look like an X.

5 Bring a large pot of water to a boil. Working in batches, drop the ravioli in the water and boil for 3 minutes or until they float to the top. Transfer gently to a colander to drain.

6 Set an extra-large skillet over medium-high heat. (The wider the surface area, the more evenly the ravioli will cook. If you do not have an extra-large skillet, do these next steps in two batches.) Add the smoked paprika butter and let it melt until frothy. Add the chickpeas and toast them in the butter for 1 minute. The butter will start to brown; that is okay. Add the drained ravioli and toss gently in the butter for 1 minute to coat and toast them.

7 To serve, put all of the ravioli on a large platter and top with the butter and chickpeas from the skillet. Squeeze lemon juice over the top, and then drizzle with the mint yogurt. Just before serving, top with the crumbled feta cheese and crumbles of the kataifi pastry (if using).

SMOKED PAPRIKA BUTTER MAKES 1⅛ CUPS

1 cup (2 sticks) unsalted butter, softened

2 teaspoons harissa (see page 49)

1 teaspoon smoked paprika

1 teaspoon kosher salt

In a mixing bowl, combine the butter, harissa, paprika, and salt, and mix completely. Store in an airtight container in the refrigerator for up to 2 weeks.

MINT YOGURT MAKES ½ CUP

½ cup plain whole-milk yogurt

1½ tablespoons chopped fresh mint leaves

Pinch of kosher salt

In a bowl, combine the yogurt, mint, and salt, and mix well. Store in an airtight container in the refrigerator for a few hours. (After that, the mint will start to brown.)

KATAIFI PASTRY

A style of phyllo pastry dough that resembles shredded wheat when cooked, kataifi pastry dough is available thick or thin, and is used in both sweet and savory dishes in the Mediterranean and the Middle East. If you can't find it, substitute phyllo dough cut into thin strips.

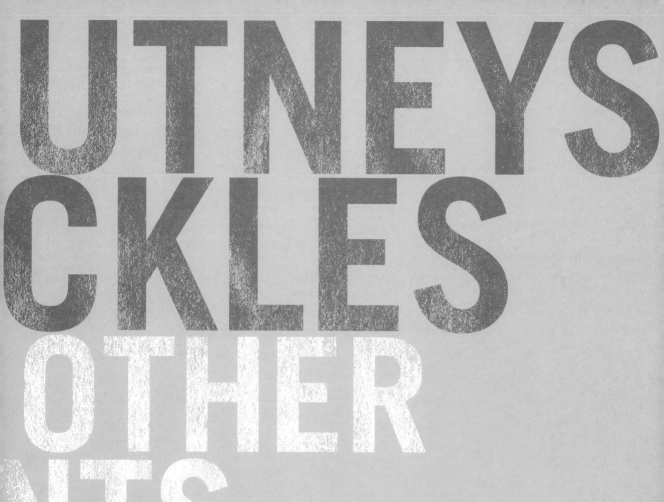

CHUTNEYS
PICKLES
& OTHER CONDIMENTS

TAMARIND DATE CHUTNEY

1½ cups Tamarind Puree
(page 173)

16 dried pitted dates

1 tablespoon olive oil

6 cloves garlic

2 teaspoons ground
cumin, toasted

¼ teaspoon cayenne
pepper

1 teaspoon kosher salt

MAKES 3 CUPS Tamarind has an unusual fruity flavor, but since it's not too sweet, I sweeten this chutney by adding dates. In India they often use a trio of flavors for a beautiful balance in a dish: some kind of sweet, often a chutney like this one; something spicy or salty; and then something refreshing like a yogurt raita. So think about using chutney in different dishes—adding it to dals, curries, fritters, and even soups. This would be great with the saag paneer on page 82, and with the curried sweet potato pancakes on page 78.

1 Put the tamarind puree in a food processor.

2 Put the dates in a small saucepan and add water to cover. Turn the heat to medium-high and bring to a boil. Once the water boils, remove the pan from the heat and leave the dates to soak in the water until they have softened, 10 minutes.

3 Meanwhile, heat the olive oil in a small sauté pan set over medium heat. Add the garlic, cumin, and cayenne and cook, stirring constantly, for 1 to 2 minutes, until the garlic and spices are toasted. Add the garlic mixture to the tamarind in the food processor.

4 Drain the dates, discarding the water, and add them to the food processor. Add the salt. Puree the mixture until completely smooth. Pour the chutney into a bowl and let it cool before serving. Stored in an airtight container, the chutney will keep in the refrigerator for up to a week.

PICKLED DAIKON RADISH

MAKES 1 QUART I think raw daikon radish is the perfect vegetable for pickling. It has a little crunchy bite, but the texture, once cooked, still has body and stands up to the vinegar better than most other vegetables. The daikon absorbs the pickling seasoning without being overpowered by it. So if you want to add some zing or zest to your dish, as well as great texture, pickled daikon is your veggie. For example, in rich fried rice, like the Waipio Valley sweet fried rice on page 89, you might want to add lightness; the daikon does that. In a salad, like the Korean chopped salad on page 50, let's say you want something that will stand up to toasted sesame oil but complement it at the same time; pickled daikon works beautifully. It almost sounds like I'm in love with this recipe, and I am!

1 daikon radish (see page 37), peeled and cut into thin strips

3 medium carrots, peeled and cut into thin strips

1 small white onion, thinly sliced

2 tablespoons canola oil

7 cloves garlic, sliced

3 jalapeño peppers, sliced

1 (2-inch) cinnamon stick

1 whole star anise

1 teaspoon coriander seeds

¼ teaspoon ground turmeric

1 cup rice wine vinegar

½ cup sugar

2 tablespoons kosher salt

1 Combine the daikon, carrots, and onion in a medium heatproof bowl.

2 In a small saucepan set over medium heat, heat the oil. Add the garlic and peppers, and cook for 2 minutes, until just before the garlic starts to brown. Add the cinnamon, star anise, coriander seeds, and turmeric, and cook for 1 minute to release their aromas. Add the rice wine vinegar, sugar, salt, and ⅓ cup water, and raise the heat to high. Bring the mixture to a boil, and then pour all of it over the vegetables in the bowl. Mix well and let cool in the refrigerator.

3 Transfer the cooled mixture to an airtight container. The pickled daikon can be stored in the refrigerator for up to 2 weeks.

CURRIED PICKLED PEPPERS

MAKES 1 QUART On one of my first trips to the ashram in Ahmednagar, India, I learned to make curried pickled tomatoes from the women who worked in the kitchen. Because there was no refrigeration at the ashram at that time, we pickled anything that wasn't cooked and eaten the same day. Some of the vegetables were pickled with curry spices. Shallots, okra, cauliflower, and chiles were all delicious— and were the inspiration for this dish. The concept of pickles is always the same: you heat up vinegar and sugar, toast some spices, and then pour everything over your choice of vegetables. When you see how easy it is to pickle at home, you'll love having different types of pickles in your fridge. You can snack on them, add them to sandwiches, and chop them up for a garnish in a bean soup with some sour cream—who knew there were so many uses for a pickle?

The peppers and chiles in this recipe are my suggestions— use your favorites or whatever is available at your local market. I like to keep a mix of mild and spicy together—the shishitos aren't spicy (usually), the California and poblano are mildly spicy, and the Fresnos and red jalapeños are quite spicy. Keep the chiles and peppers whole, unless you are using large ones that need to be cut into smaller pieces to fit in the Mason jar.

2 tablespoons olive oil

7 shishito peppers (see page 148)

3 red Fresno chiles or red jalapeño peppers

1 California or poblano chile

½ white onion, cut into thin strips

7 cloves garlic

1 cup cider vinegar

½ cup sugar

5 (1-inch) pieces fresh turmeric (see page 122), peeled and cut into ¼-inch-thick slices, or 1 teaspoon ground turmeric

1 (3-inch) piece fresh ginger, peeled and cut into ¼-inch-thick slices

4 (2-inch) cinnamon sticks

2 tablespoons kosher salt

1 tablespoon ground cumin, toasted

1 teaspoon ground coriander, toasted

1 teaspoon black mustard seeds (see page 78)

1 Heat the olive oil in a large sauté pan or skillet set over medium-high heat. Add the peppers, chiles, and onion, and cook until the onion starts to brown and the skin on the peppers blisters slightly, 3 to 4 minutes. Add the garlic and cook, stirring occasionally, for 2 minutes, being careful not to let it brown. Transfer the mixture to a medium heatproof bowl.

(recipe continues)

SHISHITO PEPPERS

A small, thin-walled green pepper that is used in both Japanese and Spanish kitchens, the shishito is 3 to 4 inches long and is found in most Asian markets or in any well-stocked grocery. They are typically mild flavored, although once in a while you'll find one with some heat. They're most flavorful when cooked, either sautéed or fried.

2 In a small saucepan set over high heat, combine the vinegar, sugar, turmeric, ginger, cinnamon sticks, salt, cumin, coriander, mustard seeds, and ½ cup water, and bring to a boil. Turn off the heat and pour this over the pepper mixture. Push the peppers down to submerge them. Let the mixture sit for 30 minutes at room temperature.

3 Decoratively arrange the peppers, then the cinnamon, ginger, and turmeric pieces, in a clean 1-quart Mason jar (or other similar container). Pour the liquid over the top to cover. Let cool, uncovered, in the refrigerator, and then close with the jar lid. The pickles will keep in the refrigerator for up to a month.

TOMATO JAM

MAKES 2 CUPS In this recipe I highlight the sweetness of the tomatoes by adding caramelized onions. Onions have more sugar than most vegetables, and by browning them you are actually bringing out their natural sugars. There are so many uses for this jam; try it with my Singapore crab cakes on page 108, the black kale on page 79, quinoa fritters, curries and rice, or on a piece of toast with fresh basil and a piece of cheese. It's the jack of all jams!

1 Heat the oil in a heavy-bottomed saucepan set over medium heat. Caramelize the onions until golden brown, 3 to 4 minutes.

2 Add the tomatoes, chile, sugar, lime juice, ginger, cumin, cinnamon, clove, and salt. Cook, stirring, over high heat until the mixture comes to a boil, 4 to 5 minutes. Reduce the heat to low and simmer, stirring occasionally so that the ingredients don't stick to the bottom of the pan and burn, until the mixture is thick and sweet, 1 hour.

3 Transfer the jam to a shallow container and put it in the refrigerator, uncovered, to cool. Use immediately, or store the jam in an airtight container in the refrigerator for up to 1 week.

2 tablespoons olive oil

1 small white onion, diced

¾ pound ripe tomatoes, cored and chopped

1 serrano chile, with seeds, chopped

¼ cup sugar

2 tablespoons lime juice (from 1 lime)

½ tablespoon minced peeled fresh ginger

½ teaspoon ground cumin, toasted

¼ teaspoon ground cinnamon

1 whole clove

1½ teaspoons kosher salt

JAPANESE PICKLED VEGETABLE RIBBONS

2 medium carrots, peeled

1 small daikon radish (see page 37), peeled

3 Persian cucumbers, peeled

5 red radishes, thinly sliced

2 cups rice wine vinegar

¼ cup low-sodium soy sauce

½ cup mirin (rice wine)

½ cup sugar

1 tablespoon kosher salt

MAKES 3 CUPS I love to make long ribbons with whatever vegetables I have on hand, so that I can arrange them—thin, flowing, and beautiful—on the plate as a side salad. These pickled vegetables are great whether they are marinated for thirty minutes and stay really crunchy, or for hours and soften up a little. Experiment and see which one you like better!

1 Using a mandoline, very thinly slice the carrots, daikon, and cucumbers lengthwise, so that they create fine ribbons of orange, green, and white. Put the vegetables in a large bowl and add the radishes.

2 In a separate bowl, combine the rice wine vinegar, soy sauce, mirin, sugar, and salt, and mix until the sugar dissolves. Pour the vinegar mixture over the vegetables and mix well to combine. Make sure that the vegetables are submerged below the pickling liquid.

3 Transfer the bowl to the refrigerator and let the vegetables marinate for at least 30 minutes. As they marinate, the vegetables will soften and sink further into the pickling liquid. Because the ribbons are delicate and will become soft and soggy over time, these pickles are best eaten on the same day they are prepared. You can use them the following day, but I don't recommend using them when they are more than 2 days old.

LEMON MARMALADE

MAKES 1½ CUPS Growing up, every Saturday night I'd sleep over at my grandmother's house, and every Sunday morning I'd run next door to my Aunt Fay's house, where she would make a "simple" Sunday morning breakfast for me: Russian dumplings with sour cream, toast, marmalade, chicken livers and onions, and scrambled eggs! The flavor of the marmalade has stuck with me, and I always think of Aunt Fay and those breakfasts when I taste this.

5 lemons, washed well
1½ cups sugar
½ teaspoon kosher salt

1 Using a vegetable peeler, remove the yellow zest from all of the lemons. Slice the zest into narrow, delicate strips and put them in a small saucepan. Cut off the ends of each lemon, and then cut down the sides, removing the white pith so that you are left with just the fruit. Discard the pith. Cut the fruit into ½-inch pieces, removing any large membrane and seeds. Put the fruit in the same saucepan with the zest.

2 Pour ¼ cup water into the saucepan and add the sugar and salt; stir well to combine and dissolve the sugar. Put the pan over medium heat and, stirring occasionally, bring to a boil, about 5 minutes. Reduce the heat to medium-low and simmer for 20 to 25 minutes, until the marmalade is thick and glossy.

3 Transfer the mixture to a container and let it cool in the refrigerator. Store the marmalade in an airtight container in the refrigerator for up to 3 weeks.

SPICY YUZU MAYONNAISE

2 cups Japanese-style mayonnaise (I prefer Kewpie brand)

2 tablespoons yuzu juice

2 tablespoons yuzu kosho chile paste

YUZU KOSHO CHILE PASTE

This Japanese seasoning is a mixture of yuzu zest, chile peppers, and salt, which is then allowed to ferment. Look for yuzu kosho in Japanese specialty markets. If you can't find the paste but can find yuzu juice, you can mix it with roasted serrano chiles and the zest of fresh limes.

MAKES 2 CUPS This mayo is a killer (and I mean that in the best way only). You can use it as a dipping sauce with a steamed artichoke, or with leftover steak for your steak sandwich. We squirt this on top of our tatsutage fried chicken at STREET (see page 94), and it's what makes people die for that dish! The flavor of yuzu is uniquely floral and more complex than fresh lime, which is more sweet and acidic. The combination of yuzu juice with the sweet Japanese mayonnaise is what makes this simple sauce exceptionally delicious. However, if you can't find yuzu or Japanese-style mayonnaise or the chile paste, use regular store-bought mayonnaise, lemon juice, salt, and any fresh chile, chopped or pureed in a blender, to create a similar result.

Put the mayonnaise, yuzu juice, and chile paste in a small bowl and whisk together until well incorporated. Store the mayonnaise in an airtight container in the refrigerator for up to 3 weeks.

KOREAN MISO
BARBECUE GLAZE

¼ cup canola oil

1 medium red onion, finely chopped

8 cloves garlic, chopped

3 plum tomatoes, chopped

1 cup canned whole peeled tomatoes with juices

1 teaspoon harissa (see page 49)

½ cup rice wine vinegar

¼ cup balsamic vinegar

¾ cup sugar

1½ teaspoons kosher salt

¼ cup sweet soy sauce

3 tablespoons dark soy sauce

⅓ cup spicy Korean miso

KOREAN MISO

This fermented soybean paste is similar to Japanese miso but is made with uncrushed beans, which give it more texture. We use a version called *gochujang,* which contains red chile peppers.

MAKES 2 CUPS   What makes this barbecue sauce different from all others is the addition of soy and Korean miso. With these ingredients, you get salt and body and a ton of flavor, making for an interesting "global" twist to the everyday sauce you might find at your grocery store.

1   Heat the oil in a heavy-bottomed stockpot set over medium heat. Add the onion and cook for 5 minutes, stirring occasionally, until it starts to color. Add the garlic and cook for 2 minutes, stirring frequently, being careful not to let it brown. Add the fresh tomatoes, canned tomatoes, harissa, rice wine vinegar, balsamic vinegar, sugar, salt, and 2 cups water. Cook for 15 minutes, stirring occasionally so that the ingredients do not sink to the bottom of the pot and burn. The liquid will reduce significantly.

2   Reduce the heat to low and add the sweet soy sauce, dark soy sauce, and Korean miso. Simmer for 5 minutes. Then remove the pan from the heat and set it aside to cool slightly for 10 minutes.

3   Puree the mixture in a blender until completely smooth. (You may need to do this in batches, depending on the size of your blender. To avoid burns when blending hot liquids, do not fill your blender more than halfway to the top, and always start by pulsing before turning the blender on high.)

4   Use immediately, or store in an airtight container in the refrigerator for up to 4 days.

GREEN SRIRACHA SAUCE

MAKES 4 CUPS I think this is the sauce that you'll always want to have in your fridge. A mildly spicy, almost fruity, herbal fresh condiment, it is fantastic on a piece of grilled fish, on roasted chicken, and on sautéed mushrooms. It's also great as a garnish for a rich soup, on top of mashed avocados with feta cheese, or as a dip for crudités. This Sriracha sauce is different from the typical red sauce you see in squeeze bottles in every Asian restaurant. I still use chiles, but I use poblanos, which give the sauce a rich, gentle heat.

1 Put roughly a third of the coconut, chiles, garlic, ginger, turmeric, cilantro, Thai basil, mint, chives, lime leaves, and lemongrass in a blender. Add all of the oil, ½ cup of cold water, the lime juice, and the salt. Puree until smooth. (You may need to pulse the blender at first so the ingredients don't catch in the blender blades.)

2 Depending on the size of your blender, you may be able to continue adding ingredients to the pureed sauce until all of the ingredients are used. If you need more space, pour half of the pureed sauce into a bowl and continue blending the remaining ingredients in batches, always using a little bit of the original sauce to start with.

3 When all of the ingredients are blended smoothly, pour the sauce into a medium bowl and stir well. The sauce can be stored in an airtight container in the refrigerator for up to 3 days.

1 cup shredded unsweetened coconut

3 poblano chiles, roasted, peeled, seeded, and roughly chopped

2 serrano chiles, stems removed, sliced (optional)

3 cloves garlic, sliced

1 (3-inch) piece young ginger (see page 209), peeled and roughly chopped

1 (½-inch) piece fresh turmeric (see page 122), peeled and thinly sliced

1 bunch fresh cilantro, leaves and stems roughly chopped (about ½ cup)

Leaves from 1 bunch fresh Thai basil (see page 109) or regular basil (about 2 cups)

Leaves from 1 bunch fresh mint (about 1 cup)

1 bunch fresh chives, roughly chopped (about 1½ cups)

4 fresh kaffir lime leaves (see page 21), roughly chopped

½ teaspoon finely minced inner stalks of lemongrass (see page 61)

1 cup canola oil

Juice of 3 to 4 limes (about ½ cup)

2½ teaspoons kosher salt

JAMAICAN GINGER HOT SAUCE

3 tablespoons canola oil

1 medium white onion, sliced

2 cloves garlic, chopped

1 (4-inch) piece fresh ginger, peeled and sliced

1 (½-inch) piece fresh turmeric (see page 122), peeled and sliced

3 whole cloves

½ star anise

½ teaspoon ground mace

1 tablespoon kosher salt

2 cups dried arbol chiles

4 plum tomatoes, charred (see step 1, page 73)

3 cups distilled white vinegar

½ cup honey

MAKES 3 CUPS Puerto Rico—not known for spicy foods—has a large Rastafarian community. When Kajsa was young and living there, she would find herself drawn to their nightly bonfires on the beaches of Cabo Rojo, where fresh oysters and clams are prevalent. That was where she had her first taste of homemade hot sauce: under the stars, listening to the music, eating the freshest seafood with a sauce full of distinctly Jamaican flavors. Mace, cloves, and anise give the sauce a licorice and floral flavor, and the honey tops it off with sweetness, so it's more complex and has more depth than the traditional red hot sauce. It's so amazing that it's now a staple in my kitchen.

1 Heat the oil in a large saucepan set over high heat. Add the onion and cook, stirring frequently, until it is soft and translucent but not colored, about 10 minutes. Add the garlic, ginger, turmeric, cloves, star anise, mace, and salt. Cook, stirring, for 2 minutes. Reduce the heat to low and add the chiles, tomatoes, and vinegar. Simmer for 25 minutes. Remove the pan from the heat and let cool slightly.

2 Puree the mixture in a blender until smooth, working in batches if necessary. (Whenever you are blending hot ingredients, make sure to leave the top slightly ajar at first and turn the blender on and off quickly, in order to let steam escape.) Pass the puree through a fine-mesh strainer into a bowl, using a rubber spatula to push it through and create a completely smooth sauce. Discard anything that the strainer catches. Add the honey and stir to combine.

3 Let cool in the refrigerator. Store the sauce in an airtight container in the refrigerator for up to 2 months.

MAKES 2½ CUPS I am a big fan of dipping sauces, so I take advantage of any opportunity to give a twist to my all-time favorite of mayonnaise, lime, and cracked black pepper. We use this in combination with the Korean miso glaze (page 156) on our chicken wings, but it can be used on its own. I'd love this sauce with potato chips, on a falafel, or with leftover turkey. Add blue cheese to it and use it to dress a salad with candied pecans!

1 tablespoon olive oil

1 (2-inch) piece fresh ginger, peeled and minced

1 tablespoon chopped garlic

1 cup mayonnaise

¾ cup sour cream

Juice of 3 limes

1 tablespoon honey, warmed

¾ cup chopped scallions, green and white parts (4 to 5 scallions)

1 Heat the oil in a small sauté pan set over low heat. Add the ginger and garlic and cook, stirring occasionally, for 1 to 2 minutes, until fragrant. Transfer the mixture to a small bowl and set it aside for 5 minutes to cool.

2 Add the mayonnaise, sour cream, lime juice, honey, and scallions to the cooled mixture, and whisk to combine. Use immediately, or store in an airtight container in the refrigerator for up to a week.

FIVE-SPICE MARINADE

MAKES 1¼ CUPS In my opinion, marinades are often too mild. You marinate something and then, once it's cooked, the flavor has disappeared and you have no idea if it was ever marinated or not. In this case, you'll get a very powerful kick from star anise, fennel, and lemongrass. On a roast, or even on a piece of chicken or fish, this marinade will shine through—that's what defines, for me, a great marinade. This recipe makes just enough to marinate one pound of meat or two (10-ounce) packages of tofu.

1 Put the lemongrass on a cutting board. Using the back of a knife, lightly tap up and down the stalk to release the essential oils. Cut off 1 inch of the root end and one-third of the stalk, down from the top, and discard. Cut the remaining stalk in half lengthwise and remove any tough outer layers. Thinly slice and then finely chop the lemongrass. This should give you 2 to 3 tablespoons.

2 Put the chopped lemongrass in a small bowl and add the coconut palm sugar, garlic, oil, rice wine, soy sauce, and oyster sauce.

3 In a spice grinder, combine the cloves, star anise, cinnamon stick, fennel seeds, sesame seeds, and peppercorns. Grind until they form a rough powder. Add this spice mix to the other ingredients, and stir to combine. Store the mixture in an airtight container in the refrigerator for up to 3 weeks.

1 stalk lemongrass (see page 61)

¾ cup grated coconut palm sugar (see page 129) or packed dark brown sugar

5 cloves garlic, finely chopped

¼ cup canola oil

3 teaspoons Chinese rice wine (see page 89)

3 tablespoons low-sodium soy sauce

1 tablespoon oyster sauce

6 whole cloves

2 whole star anise

1 (2-inch) cinnamon stick, broken

2 tablespoons fennel seeds

2 tablespoons white sesame seeds

1 tablespoon black peppercorns

BEZIRGAN, TURKEY

Eclecticism is the word. Like a jazz musician who creates his own style out of the styles around him, I play by ear. —RALPH ELLISON

We're in a creaky old van, winding our way high up into the mountains to the town of Bezirgan. The blue, blue sky above, and the farmhouses built of wood and white stone sitting in vast, dark gold fields of sesame, are reminders that I'm really in another world. The lush land below gradually gives way to a more arid climate, a landscape of fewer trees and more rocks. Envor, my guide, has promised a typical everyday lunch with some farmer friends of his, but we have to do a little hiking to get there. Once the van lets us off, we walk up a trail onto a small dirt road that is so filled with ruts I totally get why we're not driving. Occasionally we see an empty bottle on a rooftop, which, Envor explains, means there is an available daughter of marriageable age in the household. Isn't that wild?

We pass small stone homes and olive farms with wood fences, and we see peppers and dates drying in the sun. A curious family comes out to talk with us. The old man and woman and their daughter invite us in to taste their dates. The daughter seems anxious to practice her English, so she guides me around their yard inviting me to taste everything. The dates dry in the sun on large makeshift wooden tables. The heat of the sun releases their natural oils and sugar, and my first warm bite of one is heavenly. After the bright red peppers dry on lines strung between trees, they go onto huge sheets spread out on the ground to finish drying.

We get to Envor's friend's farmhouse and the most noticeable thing on the property is the barn, which comprises the first level of the house. It reminds me of a carport with the house above, but in this carport are goats, chickens, and cows. We climb up the wooden stairs and are greeted warmly by Abad and his wife, Nihat, who lead us into their small but wonderful, welcoming home. All of the Turkish homes I visited on this trip had gorgeous rugs strewn over the floors, usually overlapping each other, so that your feet never touch cold stone or wood. It makes the floors a magnificent jumble of color and pattern.

Nihat is going to cook and we will have a chance to taste a Turkish country meal. I immediately jump in to help. I want to see everything—what the marbling is in the dough, how she's rolling it and why, what kind of flour she's using, and anything else I can find out.

Apparently the women aren't given a lot of attention in Turkey, so although she is shy to start, Nihat eventually blossoms. She wants to show me everything. She practically beams sunshine at the idea of how important she has become—and to me, she really is!

We sit on the floor in front of the fire pit in the living room to make *yufka,* a flatbread. She shows me how she rolls the sesame flour with a simple wooden dowel, then drizzles pure tahini paste, made with the sesame seeds from their fields, into the dough, kneads it in, and then rolls it out again. This creates a lovely marbleized dough. She drizzles more tahini on the dough, kneads, and rolls it out flat. To one of the doughs she adds a fresh herb pesto and again kneads and rolls it flat. After they are rolled, the pancakes go into a *sach,* which is a thin, slightly curved cast-iron pan, on the fire.

We sit down at a low round table on the rug-covered floor and enjoy an amazing meal featuring the bread we just made, fresh goat cheese (from the first-floor occupants), freshly cured olives from their olive grove, and potatoes from the farm, cooked in butter from the cows. We talk, through Envor, about their lives, and I am struck that the concept of birthdays is foreign and neither of them knows how old he or she is. But I'm also taken with the beauty and simplicity of their lives. There is much peace here in the countryside, surrounded by olives, dates, and peppers, interrupted only by the occasional snort of an animal from below.

After the meal, Nihat disappears for a while and returns with these wonderful Turkish doughnuts, dipped in a syrup made from rose water and crowned with a rose hip and cardamom jam. Nihat is now so excited that she never wants the day to end. She brings out her handheld churn to show me how she separates cream from milk, and how she makes her yogurt. She sits on the floor and steadies the churn between her feet, showing me how I should do it when I get back home!

When it's time to go—which I can hardly bear to do—we bid them good-bye and begin our long walk back to the van. On the way, a motorbike balancing three people passes by. Envor flags them down—they are friends from years ago and they all talk excitedly with much laughter. He returns with a huge plastic bottle of freshly harvested pine honey. Now I am *really* ready to move here! Back at the van, we break out some of the sesame tahini *yufka* from lunch and drizzle it with pine honey that only an hour before had still been in the hive. There is an unexpected elegance in this supposedly "simple" village life and I make a mental note to try to take some of that back with me to the States.

BASIC
MIXES &

SPICE PASTES

INDIAN DRY SPICE MIX

6 tablespoons black mustard seeds (see page 78)

6 tablespoons cumin seeds

2 teaspoons fennel seeds

¼ cup ground turmeric

3 tablespoons ground coriander

1 teaspoon reshampatti chile powder or cayenne pepper

MAKES 1¼ CUPS If you add this curry spice mixture to caramelized onions, garlic, and ginger, you have the base for a simple Indian curry. Add in any cooked vegetables, like green beans, cauliflower, and/or potatoes, then finish it with tomatoes, brown sugar, and vinegar, and you have a wonderfully aromatic vegetable curry. This spice mixture will transform almost anything! You can season your chicken or fish with this dry blend before cooking and then top it with a mixture of yogurt, grated cucumber, salt, and pepper. Or top it with the tomato jam on page 149.

Put the mustard seeds, cumin seeds, fennel seeds, turmeric, coriander, and reshampatti in a small mixing bowl and stir to combine. Store in an airtight container for up to 2 months. Stir before using.

AFRICAN SPICE MIX

½ cup paprika

½ cup berbere red pepper

6 tablespoons shiro powder

1 teaspoon mitmita chile powder

1 teaspoon ground cinnamon

½ teaspoon ground turmeric

MAKES 1½ CUPS This blend of spices is great for giving an African flair to kebabs of red meats or chicken, hearty greens like collards or kale, or pulse and grain dishes like lentils or rice. We even use it as a spice on our French fries at the restaurant. Berbere red pepper is a spice mixture that has a deep, rich taste. Shiro powder is an Ethiopian blend of chickpeas, onions, garlic, chiles, and ground ginger that is used both to flavor and to thicken foods. Mitmita is a spicy powdered seasoning that is orange-red in color and contains ground bird's-eye chiles, cardamom, cloves, cinnamon, cumin, and sometimes ginger. All three of these can be found in any Ethiopian or other African market or online.

Combine the paprika, berbere, shiro powder, mitmita, cinnamon, and turmeric in a small mixing bowl. Stir together with a spoon. Store in an airtight container for up to 2 months.

MAKES 1¼ CUPS Za'atar ("thyme" in Arabic) is used to season everything from flatbreads to vegetables. The first time I tried this mixture I was working on a kibbutz in Israel. After a morning of picking pears in the field, the afternoon snack was often roasted eggplant with tahini and za'atar spice mix, and a little feta cheese. I don't know whether it was the hard work, or whether the food really was just that good, but wow. I love this spice mix sprinkled on chicken and then roasted, or over warm feta cheese served with olive bread toast points and some pickled peppers. You can buy za'atar at many Middle Eastern markets, but it's simple to make at home.

¾ cup white sesame seeds, toasted

¼ cup dried thyme

3 tablespoons ground sumac (see page 16)

Combine the sesame seeds, thyme, and sumac in a small mixing bowl. Stir together with a spoon. Store in an airtight container for up to 2 months.

THAI CURRY PASTE

MAKES 1¼ CUPS This is a paste you can make instead of buying one from the store. It will give you a light, simple, and uncomplicated curry that's fantastic. Making the paste ahead (it keeps for five days) means you can have a delicious Thai curry in a very short time. All you have to do is pull it out of the fridge, put it into a pot with fresh lime juice and coconut milk to taste, and simmer until golden. Add fish, pork, or meat, or practically any vegetable, and you'll have a wonderful meal. These flavors are used all over Southeast Asia and will give your cooking a new dimension of flavor.

1 Put the lemongrass on a cutting board. Using the back of a knife, lightly tap up and down the stalk to release the essential oils. Cut off 1 inch of the root end and one-third of the stalk, down from the top, and discard. Cut the remaining stalk in half lengthwise and remove any tough outer layers. Thinly slice and then chop the lemongrass.

2 Put the lemongrass, shado beni, Thai basil, mint, chiles, ginger, kaffir lime leaves, green peppercorns, coriander seeds, turmeric, olive oil, lemon juice, and salt in a food processor and puree until the mixture forms a smooth paste. Scoop it into an airtight container and store in the refrigerator for up to 5 days. Stir before using.

1 stalk lemongrass (see page 61)

1 bunch fresh shado beni leaves

1 cup fresh Thai basil leaves (see page 109) or regular basil leaves

½ cup fresh mint leaves

4 serrano chiles, stemmed and sliced

1 (3-inch) piece fresh ginger, peeled and chopped

10 fresh kaffir lime leaves (see page 21), chopped

2 tablespoons (about 2 strands) Thai green peppercorns in brine (see page 132)

1 tablespoon coriander seeds, toasted

2 teaspoons ground turmeric

½ cup extra virgin olive oil

Juice of 2 lemons

1 tablespoon kosher salt

SHADO BENI

An herb with long serrated leaves that have an aroma similar to cilantro, this is found most often in Asian and Caribbean markets. It can also be found under the names "sawtooth" and "culantro."

MEXICAN SPICE PASTE

4 cups fresh orange juice

Juice of 1 grapefruit

Juice of 1 lemon

1 cup achiote paste
(about ½ brick)

½ cup extra virgin
olive oil

½ bunch fresh cilantro,
stems and leaves chopped
(about ⅛ cup)

½ bunch epazote,
chopped (about ⅛ cup;
optional)

2 tablespoons kosher salt

EPAZOTE

When raw, this herb,
common to Central and
South America, has a
grassy, pungent, earthy
flavor. It's traditionally
used to flavor beans,
corn, and fish. Look for
it in Latin markets, or
substitute fresh oregano.

MAKES 3 CUPS This paste is the basis for what's known as "pibil" in Mexico. It originated in the Yucatán, and the traditional way of using it is to marinate pork, fish, or chicken in it, wrap in banana leaves with sliced tomatoes and grilled onions, then slowly cook it. Pibil is typically served with white rice, black beans, plantains, and pickled onions.

1 Put the orange juice, grapefruit juice, and lemon juice in a small saucepan set over medium-high heat. Bring to a boil. Then reduce the heat to low and simmer for 30 to 40 minutes, until the juice is thick and syrupy and has reduced to 1 cup.

2 Pour the reduced juice into a blender and add the achiote paste, olive oil, cilantro, epazote (if using), and salt. Puree on high speed until the mixture is completely smooth. Transfer it to a container and chill in the refrigerator, uncovered, for at least 30 minutes. Store the paste in an airtight container in the refrigerator for up to 1 week.

TAMARIND PUREE

MAKES 3 CUPS In countries worldwide, tamarind puree is a base for many recipes, from candies and drinks in Latin cultures to sauces and marinades in Asia. It continues to show me how closely related, through food, all of our lives really are. Food has no boundaries. It's that great equalizer in the human race.

1 Break the tamarind into smaller pieces. (It will be sticky. You can do this with a knife or with your hands.) Put it in a small heavy-bottomed saucepan, add 4 cups of cold water, and set it over low heat. Bring the water to a simmer and cook, stirring occasionally so that the tamarind doesn't stick to the bottom and burn, for 15 to 20 minutes, until the pods are soft and falling apart. Turn off the heat and use a spoon to push on the tamarind so that it breaks apart even more and is mashed into the water. Let it sit for 15 minutes.

2 Push the tamarind through a strainer into a bowl or container. (Every once in a while, you'll need to discard the fibers and seeds that the strainer collects.) It is okay if the watery liquid goes through as well. At the end you will have a very smooth paste with some water in it. Stir it together before using. The puree will keep in an airtight container in the refrigerator for up to 1 week.

1 (1-pound) package tamarind pulp, sometimes called tamarind paste

TAMARIND

The fruit of the tamarind tree is a legume, sometimes called a "pod," with a hard brown shell, which must be removed before using. Found throughout Asia, Southeast Asia, India, and in many Latin American countries, the fruit has a fleshy, juicy pulp that is best described as sweet and sour in taste.

MONGOLIAN STEPPES, MONGOLIA

Do not go where the path may lead, go instead where there is no path and leave a trail. —RALPH WALDO EMERSON

There's something crazy and strange about a "white night" in Mongolia. We're so close to the southern border of Russia that even though it's 11 P.M., it's still light out. The sky is blue, but the shadows cast by the light make it seem almost like sunset. It creates an inexplicable sense of waiting and confusion mixed with awe. And even odder still is to be in that light with that blue sky and see a luminescent full moon. The only thing more awesome is what happens next: a rainbow.

Don't ask me to explain the phenomenon; you'd be stuck with some kind of scientific light-bending, reflection-off-of-clouds explanation. And that would just steal all of the magic from the moment. But it is the most hauntingly beautiful thing I have ever seen in my life—and I'm seeing it all above my yellow tent on the side of a red mountain in the northwest steppes of Mongolia.

I'm here because I thought it sounded romantic to ride horseback through the mountains of Mongolia. I obviously had no idea what I'd find, since "romantic" is not how I would describe this trip. "Tough, demanding, and uncomfortable" would definitely fit the bill. But so would "amazing, tremendously beautiful, and wild." Two ends of the spectrum, I know. The people in this part of Mongolia are almost all nomadic; there are very few cities and no roads. Really, no roads at all. Not even paths, to my eye. The steppe is all rocky terrain, rivers, and never-ending mountains dotted with pines. Here and there pops up a lake so deeply turquoise blue you can't believe your eyes.

On the banks of a bright blue lake called Khukh Nuur, we sleep in "gers," which are the equivalent of Russian yurts, and on some mornings awaken to the incongruous sound of bells and bleating. My unconscious can't quite place it, but as I open my eyes something in me says "cowbell." Not quite. A herd of unattended sheep and goats has wandered into our campsite to graze. The goats are the most hilarious of the bunch, inquisitively standing on their hind legs to peer into the Jeeps' windows.

Breakfast sometimes consists of powdered eggs, but every once in a while we have a noodle and mutton soup called "guriltai shul." It's made up of sautéed onions and carrots, stir-fried spiced mutton, water, and fried noodles. It's pretty basic, as is everything in this wild

land, but on a cold mountain morning it tastes like a king's feast!

I'm lucky enough to be in Mongolia during the Naadam Festival, which is like a countrywide Olympics. Standing outside a tiny town called Zuungobi, we see the dirt lanes, wood structures, and a few square adobe buildings that make up the "town." The steppe above Zuungobi is where much of the festival activities take place. Three gers are set up: one for the women, one for food preparation, and the last where the children can play out of the heat. The elder women of the village are two sisters, dressed in their holiday-best maroon robes with gold piping and gold sashes, and belts with silver and turquoise buckles. While the men in our group are invited to a prayer session in order to bless the Naadam Festival (no women are allowed), the women are invited to come into the women's ger and talk. The Mongolian nomadic culture is filled with ritual, much of which our guide, Nara, has schooled us in so as not to offend our hosts. Many of the rituals have to do with which hand you use for eating (the right) and which direction you move when entering a ger (right). I don't know where all of these rules came from, but such is the way with ritual. So, as taught, we enter the ger, careful to step over the threshold with our right foot, wind to the right, and then sit. The Mongolian women follow and we all sit across from each other in a circle.

They pass a plate of soft cheese and hard cheese made with dzoh's milk. A dzoh is a cross between a cow and a yak, bred to withstand the mountain altitudes and have the tame, docile nature of a cow. They cut the oddest figures on the mountainside because you always do a double take: is it a horse? a dog? Its free-flowing mane and tail, horns of a steer, and shaggy coat are nothing like any animal I'm familiar with. And by the way, they are frisky and aggressive, unlike our cows. I made the mistake of getting too close and a beautiful dappled gray dzoh, protecting her three calves, charged me.

After the hard cheese, which has surprisingly little flavor, and the soft oozing smelly cheese, my favorite, a cup of *airag*, or fermented mare's milk, makes the rounds. Mongolia, being a landlocked and cold country with most of the population living in the untamed wild, does not have much fresh fruit or vegetables to offer. Most of the cuisine is very basic and based around meat and milk products. The nomads have become very resourceful at transforming all sorts of animal products into whatever is needed. For example, their gers are bound together with rope made of braided yak hair. Airag is another perfect example: since true Russian vodka is hard to come by, this fermented milk of a mare is the de facto wine. The cloudy white alcoholic beverage is sour and acidic, and not to the liking of most of my group—though of course I love it and could get drunk on the stuff!

Our snack served, the women now want to get to know us better. We speak using Nara as interpreter. We find out

that we are the first Caucasians they've ever seen, so they are very curious about our lives. They ask our ages and how many children we have. Audible gasps are heard when we say our ages. Their hard lives take a toll on face and body, so they have no way of understanding how we can possibly look so young. But they seem absolutely flabbergasted that some of us have no children. They simply can't comprehend it. I see that they're trying to be polite, but a couple of them exchange a comment and there's much laughter. Nara won't translate, even though she gets a good laugh out of whatever was said.

A while later, it's time to prepare a meal. The men have brought back fresh mutton, which the women mince, season with onion and garlic, then fold and press into crescents of dough. The little dumplings are steamed over the fire, and in a few minutes we have the simple Mongolian dish called "buuz," which is very similar to the Ukrainian dumplings called "varenyky."

Before we finish the meal, the men suddenly get on their horses and ride away. They're going to await the horses coming in from the race. We jump into our Jeeps and follow, eventually stopping in the middle of more flat scrubby steppe and turquoise sky, with reddish mountains in the distance. I guess I was expecting some kind of finish line. We wait for more than an hour, and suddenly, a yell! Off in the distance a dot approaches. Then another. The horses are coming in! The riders have been galloping a full thirteen miles, bareback and barefoot, through the mountains. As they pass at full speed, I'm amazed to see that they're all children no more than twelve years old. And the second-place winner is a little girl. Nara informs me that it's very rare to have a girl in the race because usually they're not tough enough.

When all the horses are in, the first five winners are lined up and the awards begin. In our country we award the rider, but in Mongolia it's all about the horse. An older man on horseback, wearing a flowing crimson robe and a pillbox hat with a point, begins a ritual song chant. He is called the "horse praiser," and I can see that he's held in very high esteem. The song is beautiful, eerie, and haunting, just like this country. And, just like this country, it seems to go on forever!

When I get home a friend asks me if I went dancing in any bars. I think about the sandstorms, the snow flurries in the mountains, where I used an Evian bottle filled with hot water from the campfire to warm my feet (yes, it melted and leaked), and the Mongolian cowboy song that Nara taught me on our nine hours on horseback (crap, that hurt) through the mountains on our way to the next campsite. I say to my friend, "There were no bars." But then I remember the one night that Nara, a couple of the women, and I got a few bottles of beer, climbed into one of the Jeeps, and loaded in a cassette tape. We drank and talked and listened to Russian disco music from the seventies until everyone else had gone to bed. I can see from my friend's look of distrust that somehow the fun and adventure of this story has been lost in translation, but suddenly I realize that the words "romantic" and "the mountains of Mongolia" actually do go together hand in glove.

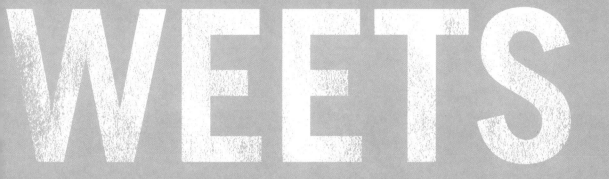

WEETS

DANISH BLACK LICORICE AND CHERRY BISCOTTI WITH BUTTERMILK KOLDSKÅL

8 tablespoons (1 stick) unsalted butter, softened

⅓ cup sugar

½ teaspoon kosher salt

1 large egg, beaten

¼ cup buttermilk

2¾ cups all-purpose flour, plus more for rolling

¾ cup dried tart cherries, roughly chopped

¾ cup soft, all-natural black licorice, chopped, plus more for serving

1½ teaspoons baking powder

1 teaspoon aniseeds

Olive oil spray

Fresh cherries, for serving (optional)

Koldskål (recipe follows; optional)

MAKES 36 COOKIES The actual name of this biscuit-like cookie is *kammerjunkere,* but it resembles the more familiar biscotti in the way it's made. Kajsa ate this in Copenhagen, dipped in a chilled soup like the one in this recipe. Denmark has some of the strongest black licorice in the world, and it comes in more than forty varieties, some salty and others sweet. Look for the real stuff at www.licoriceinternational.com, 877likrish.com, or www.economycandy.com.

Koldskål is a cold buttermilk soup enjoyed throughout Scandinavia as a dessert or snack. And while you might not think about making a soup for dessert, you absolutely have to try this during cherry season. It's divine!

1 Preheat the oven to 375°F.

2 In the bowl of a mixer fitted with the paddle attachment, beat the butter, sugar, and salt on medium-low speed until light and fluffy, 3 or 4 minutes. Add the egg and mix again until incorporated. Turn the mixer off and add the buttermilk, flour, dried cherries, licorice pieces, baking powder, and aniseeds. Turn the mixer to low speed, and then gradually turn it up to medium, mixing until the mixture comes together as a dough, about 3 minutes.

3 Put the dough on a lightly floured work surface and divide it into 3 pieces. Roll each piece into a log that is about 1 inch in diameter. Spray a baking sheet with olive oil spray and put the 3 logs on the sheet, leaving 1 inch between them. Bake for 20 minutes, or until they are just starting to brown. Remove the baking sheet from the oven.

4 Using a serrated knife, cut each log into ½-inch-thick slices (about 12 per log). Immediately put the slices back on the baking sheet (they can be closer together now),

cut sides down, and bake for 10 minutes, or until slightly golden and almost crisp (they will crisp more as they cool). Remove the baking sheet from the oven and let the biscotti cool on the baking sheet to room temperature.

5 Serve the biscotti with fresh cherries and the koldskål, if desired, for dipping.

KOLDSKÅL MAKES 3 CUPS

2 cups (about 20) fresh cherries, pitted

1½ cups buttermilk

¼ cup sugar

1 tablespoon fresh lemon juice

1 cup sour cream

1 Combine the cherries, buttermilk, sugar, and lemon juice in a blender, and puree until smooth.

2 Put the sour cream in a bowl and slowly whisk in the cherry puree. Serve immediately, or store in an airtight container in the refrigerator for up to 2 days.

MATZO CANDY
WITH CARAMEL, CHOCOLATE, AND HALVA

MAKES 11 PIECES I ate so much matzo when I lived on a kibbutz in Israel that I wasn't sure I could ever eat it again—and to be honest, unless it's loaded with butter and salt, who would want to eat this stuff in the first place? But in this recipe, the smooth, velvety texture of the halva combined with the saltiness of the cracker is the way to eat matzo going forward in life. Big statement, I know.

1 Preheat the oven to 300°F. Spray 3 baking sheets with olive oil spray.

2 Lay the matzo out in a single layer on the prepared baking sheets.

3 Put the butter, brown sugar, corn syrup, and salt in a small saucepan set over low heat. Cook, stirring occasionally, for 3 to 4 minutes, until the butter melts. Raise the heat to medium and cook until the mixture is bubbling rapidly, 3 minutes. Add the baking soda, turn off the heat, and stir. The caramel mixture will be thick and bubbly.

4 Spread the caramel over the top of the matzo crackers, covering their entire surface. Put the baking sheets in the oven and bake for 10 to 15 minutes.

5 Remove the baking sheets from the oven and immediately sprinkle the chopped chocolate over the caramel-covered matzo. Using a rubber spatula or the back of a spoon, spread the chocolate pieces so that they melt and coat the caramel matzo evenly. Then, while the chocolate is still warm, sprinkle with the halva. Let the matzo cool in the refrigerator for 1 hour or longer.

6 Break the cooled matzo into smaller pieces, and serve. Store any extras in the refrigerator in an airtight container or plastic bags.

Olive oil spray

1 (11-ounce) box unsalted matzo crackers (11 crackers)

1 cup (2 sticks) unsalted butter

2 cups packed dark brown sugar

½ cup light corn syrup

1½ teaspoons kosher salt

½ teaspoon baking soda

¾ pound semisweet chocolate, roughly chopped

¼ pound (1 cup) halva

VIETNAMESE COFFEE YOGURT
WITH CHOCO COOKIES

1½ cups brewed espresso

1 (14-ounce) can sweetened condensed milk

1½ cups plain yogurt

1¼ cups whole milk

¾ cup unsweetened cocoa powder

¾ cup all-purpose flour, plus more for rolling

8 tablespoons (1 stick) unsalted butter, softened

1 cup sugar

½ teaspoon kosher salt

1 large egg

½ teaspoon pure vanilla extract

1 tablespoon ground espresso beans

Olive oil spray

4 tablespoons cognac

MAKES 1 QUART YOGURT AND 24 COOKIES; SERVES 8 After roaming the Dong Ba Market in Hue, Vietnam, in what felt like 100 percent humidity, stopping for a delicious *café sua da* (Vietnamese iced coffee over condensed milk) or a cup of Vietnamese yogurt (a thinner, sweeter version of our yogurt) was a special treat, even if it did mean sitting with my head practically *in* a motorcycle tire! Be sure to start this recipe at least a day in advance, because it's best to let the yogurt sit overnight.

1 In a medium saucepan, whisk together the espresso and condensed milk. Heat to a low simmer (not boiling), or until a thermometer registers 115°F. Turn off the heat and whisk in the yogurt and milk.

2 Pour the mixture into a clean glass or ceramic container, and cover it with a lid or plastic wrap. Leave it in a warm place for at least 6 hours, but preferably overnight, to allow the yogurt cultures to develop. Do not shorten the amount of time you let this sit or the yogurt will not culture properly.

3 Put the cultured yogurt in the refrigerator to chill. It will thicken dramatically.

4 Meanwhile, make the cookies: Sift together the cocoa powder and flour into a large bowl. In a stand mixer fitted with the paddle attachment, cream the butter, sugar, and salt for 3 to 4 minutes, until light and fluffy. With the mixer on low speed, add the egg and vanilla extract and beat until incorporated. Turn off the mixer and add the flour mixture and the ground espresso beans. Start the mixer up again slowly to incorporate the dry ingredients; then raise the speed to medium and beat for 2 minutes, until the dough has a light consistency.

5 Turn the cookie dough out onto a work surface and divide it in half. Put a large square of parchment paper on the work surface and sprinkle it with some flour. Put one half of the dough on the floured parchment and sprinkle it with a little more flour. Cover with a second sheet of parchment, and using a rolling pin, roll the dough between the sheets of parchment until it is ¼ inch thick. Repeat with the other half of the dough. Keeping the dough between the sheets of parchment, put it in the refrigerator. Chill for 1 hour.

6 Preheat the oven to 325°F. Spray 2 baking sheets with olive oil spray.

7 While the dough is still cold, cut each half into 3 strips and lay the strips on the prepared baking sheets. You will be crumbling the cookies after cooking, so you do not need to worry about the shape they take (but you can cut them into rounds or squares if you would like to serve the cookies whole). Bake for 20 minutes. Remove and let cool to room temperature on the baking sheets. The cookies will become very crisp. Crumble them into small pieces.

8 To serve, put 1 tablespoon of the cookie crumbs in each of 8 martini glasses. Layer ⅓ cup of the coffee yogurt in next, tapping each glass lightly so that the yogurt lies flat. Top with ½ tablespoon cognac, and then sprinkle 2 to 3 tablespoons of the cookie crumbs in a thin layer over the top. Serve immediately.

THAI TEA PUDDING
WITH LIME CARAMEL AND CANDIED CASHEWS

½ cup whole milk

2 large eggs

⅓ cup cornstarch

1 quart half-and-half

1 cup sugar

¼ cup dried Thai tea mix

½ teaspoon kosher salt

Lime Caramel (page 188)

Candied Cashews (page 188)

Lime Whipped Cream (page 201)

THAI TEA MIX

This is a prepackaged blend of black tea and spices found in Thai markets.

SERVES 6 On the streets of Thailand, where the temperature sometimes soars over 100°F, there's nothing more refreshing than a plastic bag of Thai tea! Since most of the tea shops don't have seating, the Thai people take their sweetened iced tea "to go" in a plastic bag with a straw sticking out of it. The flavors of these teas were the inspiration for this dessert. The thing that makes this dish so special is the lime in the caramel, which adds an unusual tang to the sweetness. Another bonus is the crunch and spice of the cashews that are sprinkled over the top of the pudding adding a wonderful surprise.

1 Whisk the milk, eggs, and cornstarch together in a medium mixing bowl.

2 Combine the half-and-half, sugar, Thai tea mix, and salt in a medium saucepan, and bring to a boil over medium-high heat, 5 to 6 minutes. Pour the mixture through a fine-mesh strainer into a bowl, and then slowly whisk it into the egg mixture until well incorporated.

3 Wash the saucepan and then return it to the stove. Pour the tea-egg mixture back into the pan and cook over medium-low heat, whisking constantly and scraping the sides and bottom of the pan so that the ingredients don't stick and burn, until the mixture is noticeably thicker, 5 minutes. Remove the pan from the heat and pour the pudding into 6 dessert cups. Chill in the refrigerator for at least 2 hours before serving.

4 Serve topped with the lime caramel, candied cashews, and lime whipped cream.

LIME CARAMEL   MAKES 1 CUP

1 cup packed dark brown sugar

½ cup heavy cream

2 tablespoons light corn syrup

½ teaspoon kosher salt

¼ cup lime juice (from 2 to 3 limes)

1 In a deep saucepan over medium-high heat, cook the brown sugar, cream, corn syrup, and salt for 2 minutes without stirring. The caramel will start to bubble rapidly. Then swirl the pan gently to stir the caramel (instead of using a spoon), continuing to cook until the bubbles get larger and slower, 1 to 2 minutes. Turn off the heat and add the lime juice. Stir with a rubber spatula to combine.

2 Transfer the caramel to a small bowl and let it cool to room temperature. Or cover the bowl and store it in the refrigerator for up to 1 week (let it soften to room temperature before using it).

CANDIED CASHEWS   MAKES 2 CUPS

Olive oil spray

2 cups raw unsalted cashews

3 tablespoons sugar

1½ tablespoons unsalted butter, melted

½ teaspoon kosher salt

¼ teaspoon cayenne pepper

1 Preheat the oven to 350°F. Spray a baking sheet with olive oil spray.

2 In a medium bowl, toss together the cashews, sugar, butter, salt, and cayenne. Spread the mixture out on the prepared baking sheet. Bake, stirring the nuts occasionally, until well roasted, about 20 minutes. Set aside to cool.

3 Chop the candied cashews slightly before using them as a topping for the pudding or other desserts. Store them in an airtight container at room temperature for up to 3 days.

CROATIAN SOUR APPLE FRITTERS

MAKES 40 FRITTERS; SERVES 10 Called "fritule," these fritters are something between a beignet and a doughnut. On cold days around Christmastime in Zagreb, these fritters are sold at street stalls and storefronts where you can eat them warm, dusted with sugar. They almost always have some sort of candied citrus in them, which is where I got the idea to make an orange-scented sugar coating. They are a simple, unassuming pastry, but if you want to turn them into a more complete dessert, pair them with applesauce or with a Calvados (apple brandy) syrup and sour cream. It's the sour and sweet together that I just love.

1 Put ½ cup of the flour, 1 tablespoon of the sugar, and the yeast in the bowl of a stand mixer. Add ½ cup of warm water and stir with a spoon to combine. The mixture will be slightly lumpy; that's okay as long as all of the flour is moistened. Set it aside for 15 to 20 minutes, until the mixture starts to get bubbly and frothy.

2 Meanwhile, grate the apples on the large holes of a box grater. You should have 2½ to 3 cups of grated apple.

3 Put the bowl with the yeast mixture back on the mixer stand, and fit the mixer with the paddle attachment. Add the remaining 3½ cups flour, the remaining 3 tablespoons sugar, the salt, the grated apple, and half of the orange zest. Mix on low speed just until combined. Then gradually add 1¼ cups warm water, beating until the mixture has the consistency of a thick batter. Do not overmix. The dough will be lumpy because of the grated apple.

4 Transfer the dough to a clean bowl and cover it loosely with a towel. Set the bowl in a warm, but not hot, place and leave it for 1 hour to let the dough rise.

(recipe continues)

4 cups all-purpose flour

4 tablespoons sugar, plus ½ cup for dusting

1¼ teaspoons active dry yeast

3 Granny Smith apples, peeled and cored

1½ teaspoons kosher salt

Grated zest of 2 oranges

Canola oil, for frying

NOTE This dough will continue to grow and expand because of the yeast, so store it in a larger container than seems necessary. Cook the fritters within a day of making the dough—otherwise the yeast will overproof and the dough will absorb the oil while frying, leaving you with greasy fritters.

5 Stir the dough just enough to let the air out, cover the bowl with plastic wrap, and refrigerate it for at least 1 hour or as long as overnight.

6 Fill a wide pan with 3-inch sides (a cast-iron skillet works best) with enough oil to reach halfway up the sides. (Remember, the oil will expand and rise as it heats.) Heat the oil over medium heat for 4 to 5 minutes, or until a drop of dough floats immediately and a deep-frying thermometer registers 375°F.

7 Mix the ½ cup sugar with the remaining orange zest in a small mixing bowl.

8 Working in batches, drop heaping tablespoons of the dough into the oil and cook for 1 to 2 minutes on each side, until golden brown. The fritters will puff up and become very light. Transfer them to paper towels to drain.

9 While the fritters are still hot, roll them in the orange-flavored sugar until they are coated. Serve immediately.

SESAME-CRUSTED BANANA FRITTERS WITH COCONUT KAYA JAM

SERVES 6 TO 8 Walking around Singapore late at night, down by the water near a new casino, I was stuffed, having just been to four different hawker stands in a row, tasting different types of satays. I finished my last bite of a magnificent savory carrot cake and moved on to banana fritters with *kaya* jam. I wasn't expecting to be so blown away by such an unassuming dish. The combination of the grassy flavor of the pandan leaves and the sweet coconut is addictive. By the way, any fruit would go well in this jam, so if you only have pears, plums, or apples, it will still work.

⅓ cup rice flour

¾ cup all-purpose flour

1½ tablespoons sugar

¼ cup sesame seeds, toasted

½ teaspoon kosher salt

1 cup sparkling water

Canola oil, for frying

8 ripe mini bananas, or 4 regular-size bananas

Coconut Kaya Jam (page 194)

1 In a medium bowl, whisk together the rice flour, all-purpose flour, sugar, sesame seeds, and salt. Slowly whisk in the sparkling water to create the consistency of a loose pancake batter.

2 Fill a wide pan with 3-inch sides (a cast-iron skillet works best) with enough oil to reach halfway up the sides. (Remember, the oil will expand and rise as it heats.) Heat the oil over medium heat for 4 to 5 minutes, or until a drop of batter floats immediately and a deep-frying thermometer registers 350°F.

3 Peel the bananas and cut them lengthwise into long, thin slices (⅛ inch thick, about 4 slices per banana). (If you are using large bananas, cut them in half horizontally and then slice them lengthwise.) Dip each slice in the batter, drop it into the hot oil, and fry for 2 to 3 minutes on each side, or until golden brown. Transfer to a paper-towel-lined plate to drain.

4 Serve immediately, with a bowl of the jam for dipping.

NOTE One of our most
popular dishes at STREET
is made with *kaya* jam: Generously spread thick
slabs of salted butter over
toasted bread and spread
the jam on top. Top the
toast with a soft-cooked
egg drizzled with dark soy
sauce and ground white
pepper. In Singapore it's
known as a hangover cure,
eaten at any time of day!

COCONUT KAYA JAM MAKES 2 CUPS

1 cup well-shaken canned coconut milk

1 cup sugar

8 fresh pandan leaves (see page 68)

¼ teaspoon kosher salt

3 large eggs

3 large egg yolks

1 In a small saucepan, combine the coconut milk and ½ cup of the sugar.

2 Cut the root end off the pandan leaves and wash the leaves under cold running water to remove any dirt. Cut the pandan into 4-inch pieces to better fit into the saucepan. Add the pandan and the salt to the coconut milk mixture. Bring the mixture to a boil, pushing the pandan leaves down into the milk, and cook for 3 to 4 minutes until soft. Remove from the heat and let the mixture steep for 20 minutes, or until the pandan is cool enough to handle with your bare hands.

3 Pull the pandan leaves out of the pan and squeeze them over the coconut mixture to extract as much flavor and liquid as possible. Discard the leaves and set the liquid aside.

4 Bring 2 inches of water to a simmer in a medium saucepan.

5 In a stainless steel bowl, whisk together the eggs, egg yolks, and remaining ½ cup sugar. Slowly whisk in the coconut mixture. Set the bowl over the saucepan of lightly simmering water and cook gently, stirring constantly with a rubber spatula, until the mixture thickens, 15 to 20 minutes. It will seem like a long time before you see any results, but then the moment the mixture starts to set, it becomes easy to overcook—so be careful not to walk away. The texture should be like a thick custard. Pour the mixture into a clean container and put it in the refrigerator to cool.

6 Store the cooled jam in an airtight container in the refrigerator for up to 5 days.

TURKISH DOUGHNUTS
WITH ROSE HIP JAM

SERVES 6 Almost every culture has its version of a doughnut. Think about it: *churros,* beignets, *bomboloni, jalebis.* This is the classic Turkish doughnut, a basic *pâte à choux,* or puff pastry dough, with the sweet spices of Turkey. Many of the pastries I ate while traveling through Turkey were made with rose water and cardamom. After frying this batter, you very quickly dip the doughnuts in the syrup—not a soak at all, just a quick dip and onto the plate.

1 In a small bowl, sift together the flour, sugar, cardamom, cinnamon, and salt.

2 In a large saucepan set over medium-high heat, combine the milk, butter, and ½ cup water. Bring to a boil, 4 to 5 minutes. Then remove the pan from the heat and add the flour mixture all at once, stirring rapidly with a wooden spoon until the mixture is well combined and becomes one solid mass. Put the pan back on the stove over medium heat and stir continuously with the wooden spoon for 4 to 5 minutes, until the mixture is smooth. Do not shorten this step, as it is important for the texture of the doughnuts.

3 Transfer the dough to a stand mixer fitted with the paddle attachment. Mix on low speed for 2 minutes to release some of the steam. Then, with the mixer running on low speed, add the eggs, one at a time, allowing each one to be absorbed before adding the next. After the last egg has been added, use a rubber spatula to scrape down the sides of the bowl, and then mix the dough a few more times. At this point the dough will look glossy.

4 Fill a deep heavy-bottomed pot (5- to 6-inch sides work best) with enough oil to reach halfway up the sides. (Remember, the oil will expand and rise as it heats.) Heat the oil over medium heat for 4 to 5 minutes, or until

(recipe continues)

1 cup all-purpose flour

2 tablespoons sugar

½ teaspoon ground cardamom

¼ teaspoon ground cinnamon

¼ teaspoon kosher salt

½ cup whole milk

6 tablespoons (¾ stick) unsalted butter

4 large eggs

Canola oil, for frying

Rose Water Syrup (page 196)

1 cup sour cream

Rose Hip Jam (page 198)

a drop of dough floats immediately and a deep-frying thermometer registers 350°F. Reduce the heat slightly.

5 Working in batches, drop small spoonfuls of the dough into the hot oil, being careful not to splash and burn yourself. Cook for about 5 minutes, turning the doughnuts over and submerging them in the oil occasionally to ensure that they fry evenly. When the doughnuts are ready, they will be golden brown, light, and airy. If they are heavy, it means that the dough is still a little raw on the inside, in which case you can cook them a minute or two longer. Transfer the doughnuts to paper towels to drain.

6 Very quickly, dip the doughnuts in the rose water syrup and then arrange them on a platter. Serve the sour cream and rose hip jam alongside. (Or if making individual plates, spread the sour cream and rose hip jam on each plate first, and then put the doughnuts on top.)

ROSE WATER SYRUP MAKES 1 QUART

3 lemons

3 cups sugar

1 teaspoon kosher salt

1 cup rose water

½ teaspoon ground cardamom

1 Grate the zest of all 3 lemons into a medium saucepan. Then squeeze in the lemon juice, making sure to catch and discard the seeds, and add the empty lemons halves, pith and all. Add the sugar, salt, and 4 cups water, and stir to dissolve the sugar. Bring to a boil over medium-high heat, 5 minutes. Then reduce the heat to medium and cook for 10 minutes at a slow boil. The mixture will thicken slightly.

2 Remove the pan from the heat and add the rose water and cardamom. Set aside to cool. The syrup will keep in an airtight container in the refrigerator for several weeks.

NOTE Make sure that your rose hips are pure and do not have any tea leaves or other herbs mixed in with them.

ROSE HIP JAM   MAKES 2 CUPS

1½ cups (3 ounces) dried rose hips

½ cup sugar

½ teaspoon green cardamom seeds (remove seeds from pods if using whole cardamom)

½ teaspoon kosher salt

Juice of 1 lemon

1   Put the rose hips, sugar, cardamom seeds, salt, and 2 cups water in a small saucepan set over medium-high heat. Stir to combine and dissolve the sugar. Bring to a boil, 3 to 4 minutes. Then reduce the heat to low and simmer, stirring occasionally, for 20 to 30 minutes, until the mixture is thick and coats the back of a wooden spoon.

2   Remove the pan from the heat and add the lemon juice. Puree in a food processor until almost completely smooth (it will still have a little texture). Using a rubber spatula, scrape the mixture into a container and let it cool, uncovered, in the refrigerator. It will keep for up to 1 month.

EGYPTIAN SEMOLINA CAKE
WITH LIME CURD AND BERRIES

MAKES 14 INDIVIDUAL CAKES I love this cake because you can make it ahead, soak it, cover it well with plastic wrap, and still have a delicious cake two days later! Don't skimp on the lime zest, because it makes a huge difference in the cake. The amount of syrup will seem extreme, but imagine these cakes in the hot, arid climate of Egypt. The syrup is what keeps them moist and fresh.

1 In a large bowl, combine the flours, 1½ cups of the sugar, the baking powder, the baking soda, and 1½ teaspoons of the salt. Grate the zest of the limes into the bowl, reserving the limes, and then whisk the mixture well. Slowly whisk in the buttermilk until well combined. Add the butter and whisk again until smooth. Set aside to rest for 15 minutes.

2 Meanwhile, preheat the oven to 350°F. Spray two ¾-cup large muffin tins with olive oil spray.

3 Fill each muffin cup with ½ cup of the batter. Tap the muffin tins to let out any air bubbles. Put the tins on the center rack of the oven and bake for 15 minutes. Then rotate the tins and bake for 20 minutes, or until a toothpick inserted into the center of a cake comes out dry. Remove the tins from the oven and slide a small, thin knife around the perimeter of each cake to separate it from the cup and make an easy job of removing the cakes later. Let the cakes cool in the tin for about 30 minutes.

4 While the cakes are cooling, make the lime syrup: Cut the reserved limes in half, squeeze all the juice into a medium saucepan, and drop in the halves. Add the remaining 3 cups sugar, the remaining 1 teaspoon salt, and 5 cups water. Stir to dissolve the sugar. Bring the mixture to a boil over medium-high heat, about 5 minutes. Then reduce the heat to medium and cook for 10 minutes at a slow boil. The mixture will thicken slightly. Remove the pan from the heat.

(recipe continues)

3 cups semolina flour

1 cup all-purpose flour

4½ cups sugar

1½ tablespoons baking powder

1 teaspoon baking soda

2½ teaspoons kosher salt

6 limes

2½ cups buttermilk

1½ cups (3 sticks) unsalted butter, at room temperature

Olive oil spray

Lime Curd (page 201)

Lime Whipped Cream (page 201)

Fresh berries, such as blueberries, strawberries, or blackberries

5 Ladle ¼ cup warm syrup over each cake (still in the tins). Wait for the cakes to absorb the syrup, and then ladle an additional ¼ cup syrup on each one. Set aside to cool.

6 To serve, remove the cakes from the muffin tins and top each one with a spoonful of lime curd, some lime whipped cream, and a few fresh berries.

LIME CURD   MAKES 1½ CUPS

2 cups sugar

1 cup (2 sticks) unsalted butter, melted

1 cup fresh lime juice (from 8 limes)

4 large eggs, beaten

1 teaspoon kosher salt

1 Bring 2 inches of water to a simmer in a medium saucepan. Whisk together the sugar, butter, lime juice, eggs, and salt in a medium stainless steel bowl. Set the bowl over the pan of simmering water and stir gently with a rubber spatula, slowly and constantly, scraping the sides and bottom as you go but being careful not to incorporate any air. Cook for 15 minutes. The mixture will get thicker as it cooks and will eventually resemble a soft pudding.

2 Remove the bowl from the pan, transfer the lime curd to a clean container, and let it cool in the refrigerator until you're ready to use it. The lime curd will keep in an airtight container in the refrigerator for 5 days.

LIME WHIPPED CREAM   MAKES 2¼ CUPS

1½ cups heavy cream

1½ tablespoons confectioners' sugar

Grated zest of 2 limes (1 packed tablespoon)

By hand or with an electric mixer, whisk together the cream, confectioners' sugar, and lime zest in a bowl until light and fluffy. Store in an airtight container in the refrigerator.

ELIXIRS &

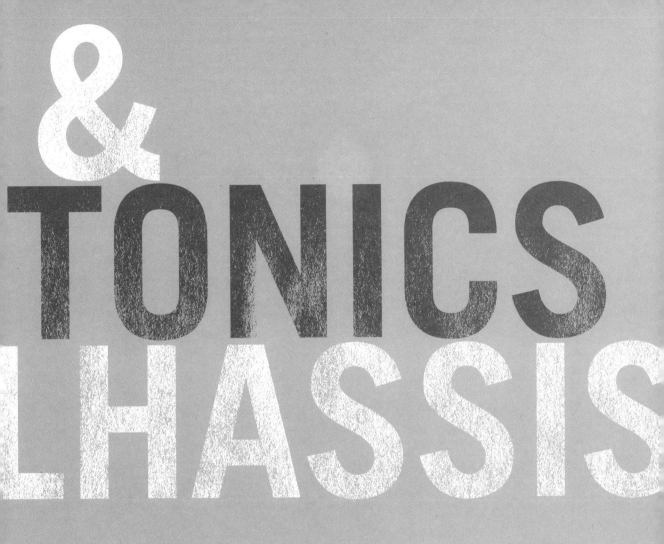

TONICS & LHASSIS

CANTON GINGER KICK

1 lemon

1 (1-inch) piece fresh ginger, peeled and minced

Ice

1 ounce (2 tablespoons) vodka

½ ounce (1 tablespoon) Triple Sec

½ ounce (1 tablespoon) Domaine de Canton Ginger Liqueur

½ ounce (1 tablespoon) Ginger Simple Syrup (page 209)

2 kumquats, cut in half horizontally (optional)

2 tablespoons chopped candied ginger (optional)

SERVES 1   When we were doing recipe testing for the opening menu of STREET, we always looked forward to the end of the session, around nine o'clock at night, when we were winding down and it was time to test cocktails! The first time we tasted this drink, created by general manager Marisa Gierlich, we muddled kumquat slices (instead of lemon slices) and garnished it with kumquats stuffed with candied ginger. If you can get kumquats, I recommend trying that because the citrus flavor is wonderful.

1   Cut the lemon in half. Cut one lemon half into thin slices and put them in a rocks glass along with the fresh ginger. Muddle the lemon and ginger.

2   Juice the other half of the lemon into a shaker, and fill the shaker with ice. Add the vodka, Triple Sec, ginger liqueur, and ginger simple syrup. Shake well and pour over the muddled ginger and lemon.

3   If you are using the kumquats, remove the seeds and push the flesh of the fruit inward so that each kumquat is cupped in the center. Stuff the cups with the chopped candied ginger, and drop the stuffed kumquats into the glass.

CANTALOUPE AND BEET
AGUA FRESCA

SERVES 4 In all the markets in Latin America, fruit drinks are everywhere—even in the tiniest town in the middle of nowhere. One of the wonderful authentic touches I discovered was a melon juice topped with beet puree. When you put a dollop of the beet puree on top of this drink, you will be blown away by how gorgeous it is and how those flavors are ideal together.

Ice cubes, for serving

1 cup Cantaloupe Juice (recipe follows)

2 tablespoons Beet Juice (page 207)

NOTE If you are adding alcohol to make this a cocktail, mix it with the cantaloupe juice before adding it to the glass. My preference here is vodka.

Put 4 large ice cubes in a highball glass and pour the cantaloupe juice over them. Using a spoon, put dollops of the beet juice on the inside edge of the glass in three places, just above the line of the cantaloupe juice. With the spoon facing the outside of the glass, push and drag each dollop of beet juice straight down the inside of the glass so that the cantaloupe juice is striped with beet juice. Serve immediately.

CANTALOUPE JUICE   MAKES 3 CUPS

½ **very ripe cantaloupe (about 1½ pounds)**

⅓ **cup sugar**

Juice of 1 lime

¼ **teaspoon kosher salt**

Peel, seed, and cut the melon into small pieces. Put the pieces in a blender and add 2 cups cold water, the sugar, the lime juice, and the salt. Puree until completely smooth. Pour into a container and chill in the refrigerator for at least 1 hour. The juice will keep in an airtight container in the refrigerator for up to 4 days.

Clockwise from left: Tamarind Ginger Cooler, Cantaloupe and Beet Agua Fresca, and Honeydew Cucumber Cooler

BEET JUICE MAKES ½ CUP

**¼ pound small red beets
(about 3 small)**   **¼ cup sugar**

1 Preheat the oven to 350°F.

2 Wash the beets well and wrap them in aluminum foil. Bake
   for 30 to 45 minutes, until they are tender when poked
   with the tip of a knife.

3 Remove the beets from the oven, unwrap the foil, and let
   them cool slightly (about 15 minutes) so that they are
   easier to handle. Then, while they are still warm, rub off
   the skins with a paper towel.

4 Roughly chop the beets and put them in a blender. Add
   1 cup cold water and the sugar. Puree until completely
   smooth. Pour the juice into a container and chill in the
   refrigerator for at least 1 hour. The juice will keep in an
   airtight container in the refrigerator for up to 4 days.

TAMARIND GINGER
COOLER

2 cups Tamarind Puree
(page 173)

1½ cups Ginger Simple
Syrup (recipe follows)

½ teaspoon kosher salt

1 (3-inch) piece candied
ginger (from Ginger
Simple Syrup recipe),
sliced

Ginger Dust (recipe
follows; optional)

Ice

Sparkling water, for
serving

Lime wedges, for serving

NOTE Want a cocktail? Add
Patrón or Chinaco tequila!

MAKES 4 QUARTS In Latin America and India, it's common to use tamarind as the base for a drink. It's hard to describe the flavor of tamarind, but I can say generally that it's extremely tangy with a slight citrus overtone. This combined with the floral essence of ginger results in an ideal beverage for a summer afternoon.

1 In a large pitcher, stir together the tamarind puree, ginger simple syrup, and salt until the salt dissolves.

2 Put the candied ginger slices in a blender, add 1 cup cold water, and puree until completely smooth. Scrape the puree into the pitcher and mix well. Refrigerate for at least 1 hour.

3 To serve, press the rim of each rocks glass into a damp towel and then onto a small plate of the ginger dust (if using). Add 3 to 4 ice cubes to each glass, and fill the glass three-quarters full with the tamarind mixture. Fill the remainder of the glass with sparkling water, and garnish with a fresh lime wedge.

GINGER SIMPLE SYRUP MAKES 1½ CUPS

1 cup sugar

1 (3-inch) piece young ginger or fresh ginger, peeled and thinly sliced

1 Put the sugar, ginger, and 1½ cups cold water in a small saucepan set over medium-high heat. Bring to a boil. Then reduce the heat to low and simmer for 30 minutes, until the mixture thickens slightly. Strain through a fine-mesh strainer into a pitcher, reserving the ginger, and set aside to cool. The syrup will keep in an airtight container in the refrigerator for up to 3 months.

2 Use the reserved ginger slices as the "candied ginger" for the tamarind ginger cooler.

GINGER DUST MAKES ½ CUP

¼ cup ground ginger

¼ cup granulated sugar

2 tablespoons confectioners' sugar

Grated zest of 2 limes

1 teaspoon kosher salt

Put the ground ginger, sugars, lime zest, and salt in a blender (make sure the blender is completely dry). Puree on high speed for 2 minutes. Store the ginger dust in an airtight container at room temperature for up to 1 week.

YOUNG GINGER

Found in Asia, young ginger has a very white, almost transparent skin, with root ends that are tinted pink. With juicy flesh and very few fibers, it is ideal for eating raw. The taste is more delicate and milder than that of mature ginger.

SPICY TOMATO GAZPACHO WITH FRESH HORSERADISH

3 cups tomato juice

1½ cups sliced pale inner ribs of celery

4 Persian cucumbers, peeled and chopped

1 red bell pepper, stemmed, seeded, and chopped

1 red jalapeño pepper, sliced

3 tablespoons grated fresh horseradish

Juice of 1½ lemons

2½ tablespoons Worcestershire sauce

½ teaspoon celery seeds

¼ teaspoon smoked paprika, plus more for garnish

1 teaspoon kosher salt

Celery salt, for garnish

Ice

FRESH HORSERADISH

This brown root, which is actually a member of the mustard family, can be found in the produce section of well-stocked supermarkets. Peel it with a knife as you might a potato.

SERVES 4 TO 6 All over Spain, when you order gazpacho in a bar, it's served in a glass like a Bloody Mary. What a great idea! The tomato juice is key in this recipe, so make sure you use the very best available. I use an all-natural organic tomato juice made by R.W. Knudsen. If you can't find that brand, substitute one of equal quality.

1 Put 2 cups of the tomato juice and the celery, cucumbers, bell pepper, jalapeño, and horseradish in a blender. Puree on high speed for 3 minutes, until completely smooth. Strain the mixture, pressing on it with a rubber spatula, into a mixing bowl; discard the solids. Add the remaining 1 cup tomato juice, the lemon juice, and the Worcestershire sauce, celery seeds, paprika, and salt. Whisk together. Pour into a container and chill in the refrigerator for at least 30 minutes.

2 To serve, press the rim of each highball or rocks glass into a damp towel and then onto a small plate of the celery salt. Put 3 to 4 ice cubes in each glass, fill with the gazpacho, and sprinkle the tops with a little paprika.

NOTE If you want to turn this into a cocktail, start with 1 ounce of Ciroc vodka (my favorite) per glass and then add the gazpacho.

HONEYDEW CUCUMBER COOLER

Juice of 2 limes

4 kaffir lime leaves (see page 21), chopped

½ teaspoon kosher salt

½ very ripe honeydew melon (approximately 2 pounds)

6 small cucumbers (I prefer Persian), chopped

½ cup sugar

Ice

NOTE Want to turn this cooler into a cocktail? Adding gin makes it the perfect summer drink.

MAKES 2 QUARTS I love cucumber in a drink—it's the most refreshing thing. At Border Grill, we make cucumber mojitos that are a huge hit. Over at STREET, we combine the sweetness of honeydew with the crispness of a Persian cucumber and end up with a drink that is perfect for a summer night.

1 In a pitcher, combine 3 cups of cold water with the lime juice, kaffir lime leaves, and salt.

2 Peel, seed, and cut the melon into small pieces. In a blender on high speed, puree small batches of the melon with some of the cucumbers, some of the lime water, and the sugar, blending until smooth, about 3 minutes. Pour into a large pitcher or container. Continue pureeing the ingredients until you have used them all up. Stir well, and chill in the refrigerator for at least 1 hour.

3 Serve over ice.

FRESH TURMERIC
AND HONEY LHASSI

MAKES 2 QUARTS One of the best Indian cooks I know is my friend Neelam Batra. She has invited Kajsa and me into her kitchen many times and shared recipe after recipe with us. We tasted a lhassi that Neelam made with saffron and pistachios, and we loved how light and fresh it was. It gave Kajsa the idea for this recipe. For this drink, I think fresh turmeric is a must.

5 cups plain yogurt

1 cup honey, warmed

4 (1-inch) pieces fresh turmeric (see page 122), peeled and thinly sliced

½ teaspoon kosher salt

Ice

1 Put 1 cup of the yogurt, 1 cup cold water, and the honey, turmeric, and salt in a blender. Puree on high speed for 2 minutes, until the mixture is smooth. Pour the mixture into a medium bowl and whisk in the remaining 4 cups yogurt and another 2 cups cold water. Chill in the refrigerator for at least 1 hour, stirring occasionally. The turmeric will gain in strength and color as it sits.

2 Serve chilled over ice.

MANGO LHASSI

4 cups canned Kesar
mango pulp

2 ripe mangoes, peeled,
pitted, and chopped

½ teaspoon kosher salt

2 quarts plain yogurt

Ice

MAKES 4 QUARTS This is the Indian yogurt drink
that most people are familiar with. I ordinarily wouldn't
recommend using a canned product, but because Kesar
mango pulp is so authentically Indian, we decided to use it in
combination with fresh mango in order to keep the distinctive
flavor. Try this over ice on a hot summer day. It's amazingly
refreshing!

Kesar mango pulp is a sweet golden pulp extracted from
the Kesar variety of mango. You can find cans of it in most
Indian markets, or substitute fresh mango.

1 Put 1 cup of cold water, the mango pulp, the fresh mango,
and the salt in a blender. Puree on high speed until the
mixture is completely smooth. Pour the puree into a
medium bowl and whisk in the yogurt and 3 cups of cold
water. Chill in the refrigerator for at least 1 hour.

2 Serve chilled over ice.

SALTED LHASSI
WITH CUMIN AND MINT

MAKES 3 QUARTS All of the elements in this drink come together to create a curiously wonderful flavor. Salted lhassis in particular are a surprise to the American palate, but they are so refreshing. Sometimes I like to add a bit of sparkling water, which makes the drink even lighter. If you have never tried one, I'd love you to try this.

1 Put 1 cup of the yogurt, 1 cup of cold water, and the mint leaves, cumin, and kosher salt in a blender. Puree on high speed for 2 minutes, until smooth. Pour the mixture into a medium bowl and whisk in the remaining 7 cups yogurt and 2 cups of cold water.

2 To serve, pour the mixture over tall glasses of ice, and garnish with a sprinkling of toasted cumin and black salt (if using) in the center of each glass.

3 Store any extra lhassi in an airtight container in the refrigerator for up to 4 days.

8 cups (2 quarts) plain yogurt

2 cups fresh mint leaves

2 teaspoons ground cumin seeds, toasted, plus more for garnish

2 teaspoons kosher salt

Ice

Black salt, for garnish (optional)

BLACK SALT

Used in India and Pakistan as a condiment, or to season chaats, chutneys, raitas, and other savory snacks, black salt is actually not black. It is a translucent brownish pink when whole, and turns light purple to pink when ground. Black salt is known for its unusual but interesting sulfurous hard-boiled-egg flavor, which is easily recognized in *chaat masala,* a common Indian spice blend.

Kajsa Alger   Liz Lachman   Susan Feniger

ACKNOWLEDGMENTS

FIRST AND FOREMOST I need to acknowledge Kajsa Alger for her dedication, talent, loyalty, camaraderie, and friendship over the many years we've worked together. Her hours of toil, generally behind the scenes, have supported me in being out there in the world, and her creative and unmatched taste buds have been invaluable to the restaurant STREET. She is the beating heart of the restaurant, and with her there, I always feel I have a true teammate with whom to share all the misery and all the excitement.

And without my life partner, Liz Lachman, I would probably be in a gutter somewhere right now. I promised her she could write that sentence, so you see what happens? In actuality, Liz is my shining star, my support system, my sounding board, and my own personal idiot. She makes me laugh more than anyone else in life and makes my life a happier place to be.

This book would not have been possible without a whole slew of people. I'd especially like to thank Mimi Morningstar, my amazing assistant, who makes order out of the cyclone that is my life and endlessly typed and retyped this manuscript; Leanne Coronel at The Coronel Group, my personal cheerleader; Andi Barzvi, my literary agent at ICM, who made it all happen; Rica Allannic, my editor, for her supreme guidance; Jennifer May, for her amazing eye; Jessica Bard and Dani Fisher, whose smiles kept the shoot a fun place to be; Laurence Dean Cohen of TLC Media Works, who always thinks outside the box; Alan Wagner, a constant spiritual inspiration and India guide; longtime creative and artistic influences Gai Gherardi, Barbara McReynolds, Su Huntley, and Donna Muir; the entire staff at STREET, who work harder than I ask, put more passion into their work than I ever expected, and make the restaurant the special place that it is—especially Marisa Gierlich, Jennifer Skochin, Christine Brashear, Jon Beckman, and Selena Ramirez; everyone at Clarkson Potter, especially Ashley Phillips, Doris Cooper, Jane Treuhaft, Stephanie Huntwork, and Christine Tanigawa; Mary Sue Milliken for saying, "Yes, let's!" all those years ago and for being my first street food comrade-in-arms; and finally, Addie Lachman for all of her cooking tips.

FROM KAJSA: To my wife and son, Celia and Seth, who gave up things that can't be replaced in order for me to do the things I love—things I won't ever love as much as I love them—and to my family and friends for their inspiration and support.

FROM LIZ: To my two mothers, Addie and Ella, who taught me equally important skills: cooking and ordering out!

INDEX

Note: Page references in *italics* indicate photographs.